God in Jesus of Nazareth

God in Jesus of Nazareth

A New Interpretation

THOMAS RONALD VAUGHAN

RESOURCE *Publications* · Eugene, Oregon

GOD IN JESUS OF NAZARETH
A New Interpretation

Resource Publications
An Imprint of Wipf and Stock Publishers
199 W. 8th Ave., Suite 3
Eugene, OR 97401

www.wipfandstock.com

PAPERBACK ISBN: 978-1-6667-2338-0
HARDCOVER ISBN: 978-1-6667-2006-8
EBOOK ISBN: 978-1-6667-2007-5

08/23/21

Contents

1

My Incarnational Muddle

LOOKING BACK ON MY own theological education I can sincerely state that I endured many classroom lectures with trepidation or noticeable disinterest. Despite the fervor and zeal of student aspirations and searching beliefs, many of our seminarian eyes glazed over when even the most gifted professor did her best to enliven terms, themes, and concepts from ecclesiastical history. It would take stamina and prayerful fortitude to endure those days or weeks where the topic was the Theology of the Incarnation in the early church. Nevertheless, it was well understood that the announced discussion topics all reflected once passionately held and boldly proclaimed profundities related to Jesus Christ. Our forebears were certain that eternal destinies revolved around these formulations and definitions.

In our classrooms were indeed heard many strange words and ancient, unusual neologisms: Gnosticism, Marcionism, Adoptionism, Docetism, Arianism, Eutycheanism, Nestorianism, Monophysitism, Apollinarianism, and others. We were told, however, that many things once firmly believed were eventually declared heretical by "Orthodox Christianity," and perhaps forever discarded. That was something of a relief! Most graduating seminarians would be hard pressed thereafter to trace the impact and ongoing relevance of these forgotten names and historical movements. It was also incontrovertibly the case that as new zealous, credentialed workers, most would look back on long or short careers and truthfully declare that these very old terms and ideas did not once overtly enter into our lives in Christian ministry.

Even if I, like the Apostle Paul, am here practicing a little foolishness (2 Cor 11:1), I do not at all intend to downplay the significance of these early leaders and movements. If they were lost in the mists and fog of ecclesiastical history, their existence pointed like an arrow to something undoubtedly monumental: the incredible creativity and spiritual energy expended in the attempt to grasp, explain, and to proclaim Incarnation as they understood it. That could not be forgotten.

I reveal this personal history in order to make a telling autobiographical point. But even as I do, I am persuaded that what I now confess could likewise be recited verbatim by countless others. I realized that though I dutifully completed my Divinity School program, I left the academy with a large "I," Incomplete. This was not for a class that required further attention before the final grade was given. It was an Incomplete in my knowledge of the very center of Christianity, the Theology of the Incarnation.

Over the next few years I came to realize that I held an unsystematic, unintegrated, rather lazy view of the Person and Work of Jesus Christ. I reflected that in seminary, I had, of course, completed formal coursework in Church History, Systematic Theology, and Biblical Studies. I had acquired useful, helpful, and essential knowledge from the obvious tasks and duties in my parish work. But analyzing each of these learning places and situations, I discovered that I had acquired only formulaic notions, snippets, and fragments of data on this eternally important subject. I could hardly state that in my theology "everything is about Jesus Christ," and that he is the spiritual center in the churches I served. I did not know enough about the Incarnation to confidently state that. As one desirous of "following Jesus," and many years after ordination "in His service," I knew well that I had to permanently re-enroll in the classroom of study, dialogue, and prayer. I had to think long and hard and continuously about God in Jesus of Nazareth.

I was encouraged in my effort by recalling remembered Scripture. The Hebrews text, 12:2, was crystal clear: "Keep your eyes on Jesus . . . ." The verse admonishes believers to view all things through the prism of our experience with the Lord. In the life of the church, there are many things to see and focus on, and pastors and leaders are often fixated elsewhere. How are we defining the Savior we are to be intently looking at? 1 Peter 3:15 also chided me: "Always be able to give an answer to anyone who asks the reason for your hope. . . ." In actuality, I needed more substantive answers for myself first and foremost.

But by far the most poignant and penetrating of all verses was that of Jesus Christ himself, as he questioned disciples at Caesarea Philippi: "But who do you say I am?" (Mt 16:15; Mark 8:29; Lk 9:20). I knew the words were not for first century followers only, but for all believers. In the very presence of the Incarnate One there could be no more stammering excuses, usual clichés, fuzzy notions. My personal goal was to provide an answer worthy of my training and position, but most of all as a reflection of heartfelt gratitude for an opportunity to even attempt to be a disciple of Jesus Christ.

I had intuitively, if unselfconsciously, known all along that the Theology of the Incarnation is a challenging discipline, filled with wonder and awe, mystery and miracle, question and incompletion. In fits and starts, I have since then gathered many thoughts and ideas, and herein I share some of the results from what will be, I believe, an eternal quest and adventure for me and for us all. There is much to learn.

2

Introductory Comments

I HAVE NO INTEREST in presenting, debating, or arguing against positions and interpretations which differ from mine. My single goal is to attempt a careful, cogent presentation of my own particular views. However, anyone dealing with the Theology of the Incarnation and its two component parts, Christology and Soteriology, is automatically enmeshed in two thousand years of Christian Historical Theology. Every new study, therefore and of necessity, draws on that massive literature and legacy. Even so, depthful historical review is not required when individual interpretive studies, such as mine, are offered.

Here, I will draw very selectively on that long theological tradition, recognizing, of course, the New Testament as polar star. My approach to Biblical Studies is historical-critical, but my conclusions are generally conservative. I will utilize and refer often to two indispensable Creeds of the church, those of Chalcedon (451 CE) and Constantinople (681 CE).

From the writings of the Apostle Paul and from the Confessions of the Reformed Tradition, I glean my basic understanding of the Sovereignty of God, the foundation of Incarnational Theology. I affirm that this Sovereignty is not demonstrated by mechanistic outcomes, but by the absolute wisdom and power of God to effect and ensure those desired outcomes. God is unquestionably able to produce the latter without an absolute predestining of either persons or events. In line with these views it will become apparent that I profess belief and faith in God's mysterious Election of Grace. But as a confirmed Christian Universalist, I roundly denounce the odious notion of an Election of Reprobation.

Following my previous writings, this is also a book exclusively of essays. Intentionally, they build upon each other as things unfold, but can be studied independently. I have taken pains to prevent redundancy in details, though there is some of that to create context. There is a large number of essays, mostly short and hopefully concise. Though I owe many things to many people, this is not a research project, but does contain footnotes and bibliography. The pages reflect my personal summations only.

In the next essay, I give a lengthy outline of what I call Foundational Principles. Here, I present what I posit as three irreducible realities of the Christian faith.

1. Its fundamental teaching is that every person is now, and will forever be, in an inseverable relationship with the Blessed Holy Trinity.
2. The Incarnation is a gracious, loving gift from the Holy Trinity to effect and affect the temporal and eternal outcomes of this divine-human relationship.
3. The Holy Trinity will orchestrate such outcomes, for persons and the cosmos, according to the divine sovereign will, whose primary attribute is agape Love.

I approach the entirety of this topic utilizing three Hermeneutical Norms, formulated in question form.

1. Why did God choose Incarnation as a self-expression?
2. What does God experience in Incarnation?
3. What does God accomplish in, by, and through Incarnation?

As a whole, this book provides my answers to these questions.

3

Foundational Principles for the Theology of the Incarnation

THE CONTENTS OF THIS book can be contextualized by reference to what I now present as Foundational Principles. I have penned clarifying essays on some of the Principles, but everything written here can be referred to these seventy-eight items. To interpret them and the essays comprehensively, I employ, tacitly and without comment, the three Hermeneutical Norms from the last chapter.

1. Belief in God as Blessed Holy Trinity is a mysterious act, itself a gift wholly from God, the believer contributing nothing to the process.
2. All knowledge of God derives from gracious, ongoing revelations of Godself to humanity.
3. Since God does not simultaneously provide both revelation and interpretation, every revelation must therefore be interpreted.
4. The writings of Holy Scripture, and all human interpretations of divine revelation, are therefore always speculative.
5. The ambiguous nature of God's self disclosures limits human understandings of divine reasons for Incarnation.
6. Faith communities must engage in ongoing dialogue to obtain consensus understanding and interpretation of divine revelations.

7. Faith communities must intentionally attempt to identify any divine revelations in Holy Writ.

8. Christian Historical Theology is a record of the diversity of interpretation of revelations from God, particularly those identified in Holy Writ.

9. God in Godself is an ultimate mystery, but has self disclosed to believers in such non-literal terms as "Blessed Holy Trinity," "God in Three Persons," "Father," "Son," "Holy Spirit," et alia.

10. Blessed Holy Trinity has revealed itself as an eternal, all-loving intrapersonal and interpersonal relationship.

11. The intrapersonal deliberations and actions of the Holy Trinity are unknowable except as they have been revealed in self disclosure.

12. Trinity as interpersonal has revealed the desire for an eternal, loving interpersonal relationship with all human persons.

13. Endowment of "personhood" on any human creature is an act wholly of God.

14. In eternal intrapersonal counsels before the Creation, Blessed Holy Trinity chose to utilize Incarnation as a unique medium through which to communicate divine teachings and to accomplish divine intentions related to all humanity and to the cosmos.

15. Incarnation in no way diminishes or affects the divine attribute of immutability.

16. Belief in the Incarnation is a mysterious act, itself a gift wholly from God, the believer contributing nothing to the process. No one can call Jesus Lord except by the Spirit of God (1 Cor 12:3).

17. Incarnation is a mysterious, gracious, loving act, wholly of God, humanity contributing nothing to the originating and ongoing Union.

18. The writings of the New Testament are an interpretive witness to human encounters with the Incarnation.

19. The writings of the New Testament do not provide wholly inclusive definitions of either the Person (Christology) or the Work (Soteriology) of Jesus Christ.

20. The writings of the New Testament do not provide a guide for applying, interpreting, and understanding the many variegated Christological and Soteriological titles for Jesus Christ.

21. Christian Theology has produced one consensus ecumenical definition of Christology, the Creed of Chalcedon (431 CE), which was supplemented by the Creed of Constantinople (681 CE).

22. Christian Theology has not produced a consensus definition of Soteriology, how Jesus Christ actually "saves" persons.

23. The God of the Incarnation is the same God revealed in the signal events of the Old Testament: Creation, Call of Abraham and Sarah, Exodus, Giving of the Law, Settlement of the Promised Land, Sending Prophets.

24. In the Incarnation, God completes the mandate unfilled by Israel, to "bless all peoples of the earth."

25. The Incarnation occurred within the narrow socioreligious context of first century Israel, but its meaning and interpretation are not thereby confined to that context.

26. Interpretations of the Incarnation cannot be limited to Jewish or to Christian Theology.

27. Christian Theology must attempt to determine and to share the implications of the Incarnation for all peoples and all world religions.

28. In the "fullness of time," as determined by God, the Second Person of the Trinity, revealed as "Son of God," became Incarnate in a single, historical human being, Jesus of Nazareth.

29. Christian Theology must ascertain any relationship between the Theology of the Incarnation and the birth of Jesus Christ.

30. In the Incarnational Union, Jesus of Nazareth was a historic Jew, but God, the Second Person of the Trinity, was not.

31. The Incarnation was a Union of God and humanity in one concurrent Personal Presence and one Personal Identity, not a dyad or a blending of properties, which would create another distinct entity altogether.

32. In the Incarnational Union, the Second Person of the Trinity remains forever wholly God, and Jesus of Nazareth remains wholly human.

33. The Second Person is truly God and is to be worshipped as God; Jesus of Nazareth is not God and is not to be worshipped as God.

34. Though confessing one concurrent Personal Presence and Personal Identity, Christian apperception can discern differentiating properties of God and humanity.

35. Some texts of Scripture speak of an interchange, blending, or confusion of the properties of God and humanity.

36. This imprecision can be noted in numerous texts, which speak of, for example: the Son of Man coming down from heaven; God becoming flesh; God being born; God dying on the Cross.

37. Believers may employ such Biblical language while recognizing that there is no interchange of properties, and that the words are not literally true.

38. Christian Theology confesses that the intrapersonal relationship between the Second Person and Jesus of Nazareth is mystical and miraculous, largely unknowable to believers.

39. While remaining forever wholly God in the Incarnational Union, the Second Person mysteriously experiences the entire human life of Jesus of Nazareth.

40. In the Incarnation the Second Person experiences the Jewish life of Jesus of Nazareth.

41. Christian Theology has no revelation regarding ways in which the Second Person actually influences or interacts with Jesus of Nazareth enabling him to, for example, interpret Scripture, perform mighty acts, understand his peers, overcome all temptation to achieve a sinless life.

42. Christian Faith confesses that the Incarnate Jesus Christ manifests two natural wills, at times appearing to, but not opposing each other, the "human will" always and mysteriously subject to the "divine will."

43. In the Incarnational Union, the Holy Trinity enables and facilitates the accomplishment of a single, sinless, perfect, holy life.

44. In a single life, the Incarnate Union achieves and demonstrates holy perfection in faith, trust, obedience, worship, service, and love.

45. In the concurrent Personal Presence and Personal Identity, Jesus of Nazareth dies on the Cross in complete sinlessness.

46. On the Cross, Jesus of Nazareth dies, but the Second Person, as God, cannot and does not die.

47. The sinless perfection of Jesus of Nazareth is in no sense his own autonomous achievement, but is a miraculous work facilitated by the mysterious power of God in the concurrent Union.

48. Christian Faith has no revelation regarding the relationship between the Second Person and the physically dead Jesus of Nazareth, entombed for "three days."

49. After the death on the Cross, and discovered by disciples on "Easter Sunday," Holy Trinity grants a literal Resurrection to Jesus of Nazareth.

50. Resurrection is an act wholly of God, the dead Jesus of Nazareth contributing nothing to the process.

51. Belief in the literal Resurrection of Jesus of Nazareth is a gracious, loving gift, wholly from God, the believer contributing nothing to the process.

52. Because both are acts wholly of God, Christian Faith posits the indissoluable relationship between the Incarnation and the Resurrection.

53. This relationship is not clearly elucidated in either the New Testament or in Christian Theology, but is somehow integral to divine governance of the world and the cosmos.

54. Divine revelation affirms that God will provide a literal Resurrection from death for all persons.

55. Since there is nothing inherent in human nature to procure life beyond physical death, any Resurrection of any created being is a gracious, loving act, wholly of God.

56. Christian Theology is unable to definitively interpret the relationship between the Resurrection of Jesus of Nazareth and the general Resurrection of any other persons.

57. Christian Faith asserts that in the Resurrection, the Second Person forms a radically new Union with Jesus of Nazareth, providing a Resurrection embodiment and a divine empowerment for the accomplishment of subsequent events.

58. Christian Faith cannot articulate, analyze, or describe the new Union between the Second Person and the One who was Resurrected, who appeared thereafter to disciples, "ascended into heaven," and was then "seated at the right hand of God ."

59. Nevertheless, Scripture, Christian Faith and devotion, have reflected belief that the new Union was eternalized, and that accordingly the Second Person will forever be "in" Jesus of Nazareth, in a mystical, unfathomable relationship as One who is known as the Risen Lord Jesus Christ.

60. Christian Theology does not assess the eternalization of this new Union as a diminishment or declension of divine power, nor in any way compromising the divine attribute of immutability.

61. In the new Union, the Holy Trinity freely and lovingly creates an eternal relational dimension with and for humanity, reflected in Biblical texts such as, "I am with you always."

62. Christian Faith understands this eternal Union salvifically for persons, in that the One who lived a perfect, holy, sinless life is the Risen Lord Jesus Christ.

63. As such, the Lord Jesus Christ is now and forever the perfect example, guide, model, Mediator, and "Savior" for all humanity.

64. Through the achievement of the one sinless, perfect life, Blessed Holy Trinity defines and accomplishes its eternal goal of an Atonement, an At-One-Ment, between God and humanity.

65. Now eternally including a Mediator "acquainted with our common humanity," the Blessed Holy Trinity lovingly dispenses needed, appropriate, individualized grace to all open to receive it.

66. Through the eternalized Atonement, all human beings are now, by divine fiat, "justified through the redemption which is in Jesus Christ," for "one man's act of righteousness leads to acquittal and life for all persons."

67. Christian Faith recognizes that several verses in Scripture imply a Second Coming to earth of the Lord Jesus Christ.

68. Some verses suggest an end time cataclysmic event, at which all persons will "appear" before God.

69. Even though these verses do not provide a unified event analysis, and cannot be harmonized, Christian Faith teaches a "life accountability" before God.

70. The holiness of the Blessed Holy Trinity precludes every manifestation of sin and evil from the ultimate, eternal environment to be indwelled by God and all redeemed persons.

71. Through the eternalized and universalized Atonement, all persons must progress to finally become "perfect as your Father is perfect," "children of the Most High," "children of God."

72. The example, pattern, and model for human achievement of this holy perfection is and forever will be the Mediator, Jesus Christ.

73. Since "salvation is of the Lord," all individual progression to perfection will be facilitated wholly by God, who will "finish the good work God has begun."

74. Any consummation or end for the earth and the cosmos is wholly the action of God, humanity contributing nothing to the process or event.

75. Eternal salvation occurs for any and all persons only when God's word-deed pronounces it.

76. Because of God's self revelation as eternal agape Love, culminating in the Incarnation, Christian Faith envisions and affirms a hopeful, beatific destiny for all persons.

77. By divine decree, human response to the Incarnation, temporally and eternally, will lead to personal, individual perfection and holiness, never to separation from, or "damnation" by God.

78. Christian Theology and Faith understands and interprets the Incarnation as the Foundational Principle in God's goal of ultimate salvation for all persons.

4

Two Vital Creeds

IT IS ESSENTIAL TO remember that Creeds serve very important theological and spiritual functions. One, they exist as a guide, a "key," to assist in interpreting the Scriptures. Two, they provide what the Church Fathers considered correct, "Orthodox" language for a pure, exact confession of faith among believers, most often in corporate worship. Three, they offered a succinct catechetical formula for instruction in spiritual things.

For over four hundred years, the church had struggled and grappled with heresies related to definitions of Incarnation. In 451 CE the magnificent Creed of Chalcedon was approved to help clarify faith expressions. But two hundred-thirty more testy years ensued before some absolutely necessary language was added to its language in the Creed of Constantinople, 681 CE. While believers are forever grateful to ecclesiastical leaders for their perspicuity and diligence, it is surely the mysterious presence of the Holy Spirit which must be acknowledged as the guiding hand in the sometimes petty, angry, duplicitous Conciliar transactions which lead to such profound documents.

THE CREED OF CHALCEDON

The one and only ecumenical definition of Orthodox Christology is the consensus Formula of the Council of Chalcedon. (Of course, the church has never produced such a creedal formula for Soteriology.) The Creed:[1]

> Following, therefore, the holy fathers, we all with one voice teach confession of one and the same Son, our Lord Jesus Christ: the same perfect in Godhead, the same perfect in humanity, truly God and truly human, the same with a rational soul as well as a body. He is of one indivisible essence with the Father in regard to his Godhead, and also of the same essential nature with us in regard to his humanity—like us in all respects apart from sin: before the ages begotten of the Father in regard to his Godhead, and in the latter days, for us and for our salvation, born of Mary the Virgin God-bearer in regard to his humanity. He is one and the same Christ, Son, Lord, Only-begotten, made known in two essential natures, without confusion or alteration and without division or separation. The distinction between essential natures is in no way removed because of the union, but rather the differentiating properties of each essential nature are preserved, both concurring into one Personal Presence and one Personal Identity. He is not parted or divided into two personal presences, but is one and the same Son and Only-begotten God the Logos, the Lord Jesus Christ, even as the prophets from of old and the Lord Jesus Christ himself have taught us concerning him, and as the Creed of the Fathers has handed down to us.

THE CREED OF CONSTANTINOPLE

This Council addressed the question of whether the two natures have two separate wills. Some heresies taught that only one will was present, and the Creed rejected that notion summarily. The Creed:[2]

---

1. This uncopyrighted translation, *The Creed of Chalcedon,* made by the late Charles K. Robinson of Duke University. I have edited it for this publication.

2. This uncopyrighted translation, *The Creed of Constantinople,* was published by Christia File Archives. I have edited and abbreviated it for inclusion here.

We also proclaim two natural willings or wills in him and two natural operations, without separation, without change, without partition, without confusion, according to the teaching of the holy Fathers—and two natural wills not contrary to each other, . . . but his human will following, and not resisting or opposing, but rather subject to his divine and all-powerful will. For it was proper for the will of the flesh to be moved naturally, yet to be subject to the divine will. . . . As Gregory the divine says: "His will, as conceived of in his character as the Savior, is not contrary to God, being wholly divinized." We also glorify two natural operations in the same our Lord Jesus Christ, our true God . . . that is, a divine operation and a human operation. . . . Leo most clearly says: "For each form does what is proper to it, in communion with each other; the Word, . . . performing what belongs to the Word, and the flesh carrying out what belongs to the flesh." We will not therefore grant the existence of one natural operation of God and the creature, lest we should either raise up into the divine nature what is created, or bring down the preeminence of the divine nature into the place suitable for things that are made. For we recognize the wonders and the sufferings as of one and the same person, according to the difference of the natures of which he is and in which he has his being . . . . Preserving therefore in every way the unconfused and undivided, we set forth the whole confession in brief: believing our Lord Jesus Christ, our true God, to be one of the Holy Trinity even after the taking of flesh, we declare that his two natures shine forth in his one Personal Identity; in which he displayed both the wonders and the sufferings through the whole course of his dispensation, not in phantasm but truly, the difference of nature being recognized in the same one Personal Identity by the fact that each nature wills and works what is proper to it, in communion with the other. On this principle we glorify two natural wills and operations combining with each other for the salvation of the human race.

5

Items in Incarnational Theology

THE INCARNATION WAS AND is the central event in the history of the world and the cosmos, including its final consummation. Interpreting Incarnation and discovering its implications must be a primary, foundational task of all Christian Theology.

As taught in the Scriptures of both the Old and New Testament, God is God of the entire cosmos, limited in no way by God's relationship to, or activity with, any tribe, nation, or religious group. God is at all times lovingly active among the collective peoples of the world. Accordingly, the Incarnation as an act of God, is a gracious gift to all humanity. In all its deliberations and conclusions Christian Theology must be ever cognizant of this reality.

Given its cosmic dimensions, the Theology of the Incarnation cannot be the "sole possession" of any so-called Orthodox Christianity. Historically, however, the Christian Church has tacitly claimed such ownership, and has thereby confined and defined interpretations of Incarnation within its evolving theologies. There are many facts which militate against this exclusive approach. Among them are the following.

Incarnation should not be interpreted and presented as a mere derivative of Old Testament Theology, New Testament Theology, or historical theology arising within the Christian Church. In point of fact, all Old Testament accounts of a "Coming Messiah," and all New Testament accounts of the actualized Incarnation, are incomplete and cannot be harmonized. Therefore, they are quite inadequate for a definitive Christian Theology of Incarnation with its two component doctrines, Soteriology and Christology.

In its historical social and religious context, it was inevitable that the nascent church borrow from the Old Testament in order to understand the Person and Work of Jesus Christ. Much of his self-understanding derives from selected Old Testament passages. In the Concurrent Union, Jesus of Nazareth was decidedly a Jew. However, the Second Person of the Trinity, the Son of God, was not. The Incarnate Jesus Christ was also, of course, not to be labelled a "Christian," contemporaneously, nor by any theology subsequently formulated by the church.

The writers of Christian Scripture borrowed generously from the Old Testament, particularly from Jewish Cultic Theology, in order to understand Incarnation, especially the Work of Jesus Christ. But he himself had announced that his life and ministry belonged to the entire world, in the same sense in which the Holy Trinity is God of all peoples, times, and places. This is a fundamental teaching of both Testaments. Given these indisputable facts, it must be the safe conclusion that the Triune God did not intend for Incarnation to be understood, interpreted, or proclaimed exclusively in terms of Old Testament concepts and language.

A second aspect of this consideration is to probingly inquire into the very nature of the church itself. While at the Last Supper Jesus Christ, with his dwindling flock, suggested and implied an ongoing fellowship for believers after his impending death, he neither defined nor described it. His lifelong and main emphasis was noticeably on believers worshipful fellowship in, and expanding the borders of, a loosely defined "Kingdom of God." Such a community was most certainly not defined exclusively by, and included wholly in, the many developing historic churches. Though the latter in aggregate may be part of God's larger Kingdom, and can and do mediate divine grace, the church and the Kingdom of God cannot be equated. The grace, presence, and power of God in the Incarnation are always abroad in the entire wider world, and in no way confined, or wholly interpreted, by activities and pronouncements of the Christian Church.

If the Theology of the Incarnation demands a more universal, cosmic interpretation, what is the role of the larger Christendom in that process and presentation? Several things come readily to mind.

1. The church must acknowledge that for two thousand years it has been the custodian and gatekeeper for almost all theological reflection on the Incarnation. This fact has produced a self-reflexive approach to both Christology and Soteriology, and has largely defined the intellectual and spiritual boundaries within which the subject could be legitimately discussed. Very little input has been accepted from non-Christian sources.

2. While holding fast to its historic heritage, the church must free itself from the mindset that demands exclusive interpretive use of Judeo-Christian themes. Creatively and boldly redefining and reimagining the Person and Work is a basic starting point.

3. The church must continuously articulate and demonstrate the existential relevancy of Incarnation to the lives of all persons in all socioeconomic circumstances. This is surely part of any Biblical definition of Evangelism: showing and witnessing to how an Incarnate One relates to the lives actually being lived everywhere, by all people, in "the real world."

4. Evangelism thus defined encourages Christian believers to assertively and comfortably seek out and engage in constructive dialogue with both non-Christians, and especially, with followers of other world religions. The tone and tenor of this dialogue are found in the New Testament teachings on interpersonal relationships and unswerving, loving concern for the "other."

5. From such contacts, Christian Theology can discover amazing, hereto unthought-of new vistas and horizons, and thus develop new messaging for its Good News. Expressing these new things is the responsibility and privilege of Christians in every walk of life.

6. The church must realize and accept that all interpretations of Incarnation, including its own, are necessarily speculative and

are therefore ultimately incomplete. This fact is the impetus for open dialogue with others, humbly undertaken.

7. The church must constantly review and analyze its doctrinal theology to ensure that every teaching is centered in the Theology of the Incarnation. All doctrines and beliefs not so grounded will likely be found to exist only to support and sustain the power of ecclesiastical institutions. Additionally, many doctrines may be, in fact, irrelevant or even antithetical to Incarnational Theology.

8. The God of the Incarnation adamantly objects to any church or ecclesiastical body arrogating to itself the right to pronounce on eternal destinies by reference to its own teaching, liturgy, traditions, human personnel, or dogma. This is a major, long-standing historical problem.

9. All believers in Jesus Christ may reverently and devotionally speculate on matters related to Incarnation, heavily relying on the guidance of the Holy Spirit, and on dialogue within larger faith communities. The conclusions, however, must demonstrate that Incarnation is a manifestation of an indiscriminate, eternal love for all persons, who are, by definition, beloved children of God.

10. The Incarnation contains vital, clear teaching on judgment, sin, and amendment of life, all of which are ultimately viewed through the intense, correcting power of agape love.

11. It is always, and crucially, important for the church to attempt to discover and defend "Orthodox" views of the Incarnation. Since not every definition of Incarnation can be approved, the community of faith must attend to this issue with diligence and wise discernment.

6

Brief Outline of Universalism

IN THESE ESSAYS I am attempting to demonstrate that the Theology of the Incarnation is, quite obviously, an integral part of the larger Doctrine of God. Here I will posit that the latter includes this larger hope of Universalism, since the Blessed Holy Trinity is self-equated with agape Love. I will now present my views on an exclusive Christian Universalism, since the latter term is often used by others with no reference to an Incarnation.

The Triune God created the cosmos, and, in time, created the human race to be one of the myriad occupants of this particular planet, Earth. God will direct and oversee this Earth, and will orchestrate any consummation involving it and the cosmos. In creating humanity, God's ultimate goal is to graciously and lovingly give each person life in God's presence.

As Creator, God rightfully maintains an eternal claim on the life of every individual person, and makes legitimate demands for each one relative to that ultimate redemption. God's irrevocable demands are these: "Be ye holy. Be ye perfect." God demands holy perfection, the achievement of which cannot, of course, be accomplished by any human creature in this lifetime.

However, God, in pure, free, sovereign grace, effects the mystery of an Incarnation, whereby God-in-Jesus Christ miraculously and exemplarily accomplishes one unique, perfect, and holy life. Thereafter, God eternalized that miracle for the redemption of the entirety of the beloved human race. Jesus Christ becomes the perfect Atonement, the author and finisher of all believers' faith.

The requirement for individual perfection is not thereby mitigated or removed in any way. Since a holy, perfect state cannot be achieved temporally, God graciously provides worlds and contexts in the Age to Come, where, through God's parental guidance, such perfection can become a reality. Individual "souls" go into God's eternal presence only after achieving perfect holiness in the image of Jesus Christ, and only at God's welcoming bidding.

Universalism is the most ethically demanding of all Christian Theologies for the single reason that God will never abandon, "write off," destroy, or damn any human person, all of whom are created in God's own image. Accordingly, it teaches and insists that none can ever treat another human as irretrievable, dispensable, or "lost." Universalism affirms the timeless nature of every interpersonal relationship, and that God's final, divine realm most assuredly includes all. That heavenly environment actualizes, at last, the ultimate reality of a fellowship wherein everyone lovingly relates to the other. Awareness of this eschatological state must inform all temporal, earthly interaction. God's unalterable, irrevocable demands will not be compromised.

Universalism's final cosmic vision is quite simple: God loving all; all loving God; all loving all.

It must be remembered that Universalism does not INCLUDE Incarnation; Incarnation itself produces the Doctrine of Universalism, which reflects the Doctrine of God, who is agape love.

It is easily demonstrable that not all persons welcome the idea of Universalism. The reasons for this are many, ranging from views on Bible teaching, to judgmentalism, self-righteousness, pride, prejudice, or sheer indignation that "those people" will be saved eternally. Christian Universalism is, nonetheless, true.

Some years ago, I completed a book-length manuscript which I did not submit for publication. I chose the title "Condemned to Salvation." To this day, I find that a useful, correct way to think of eternal destinies and outcomes. We will be saved because the Lord God has spoken it, and we will be saved on God's terms alone. We are, as I say, condemned to salvation. What a glorious condemnation!

Witness the Apostle Paul. This Pharisee was en route to Damascus, sincerely believing that destroying Christianity and executing Christians was the conscientious and righteous thing to do. He was a very religious man, self-described as always "keeping the law." He demonstrates the limitations of the curious notion, "Let your conscience be your guide." Jesus Christ had other plans for this gifted, passionate legalist. In his conversion story, importantly told three times in the Book of Acts, the Savior appears and addresses Paul directly. His words are eternally valid, for they are personally instructive to and for every individual. The Lord declares, "It is hard for you to kick against the goads" (Acts 9:5). For Paul it was futile and pointless to "kick against," to resist, the Savior and the new Gospel. He could not do it; God's grace would not permit it. Now chosen by God, he became a devout believer. The rest is, of course, history, and this exceptional, brilliant man became the second most influential personage on the pages of church history.

A Universalist friend once said, "You can hold your breath only so long." He was employing the same image and metaphor. At some point, in time or eternity, we will surely "come to ourselves, arise, and go to our Waiting Father" (Luke 15:16–18). The writer of 1 Timothy declared himself the "chief of sinners," but then proclaimed that, despite the sin, "God is the Savior of all, especially of those who believe"(1:15; 4:10). And the great persecutor of Christians, Paul, in a panoramic vision of the purifying, saving power of agape love, saw a day when "every knee would bow, and every tongue confess that Jesus Christ is Lord, to the glory of God the Father" (Phil 2:10–11).

Truly, wherever we are in life, we are all on a Damascus Road, and will, soon or late, meet the Risen Savior, Jesus Christ. "Neither life nor death . . . nor anything, can separate us from the love of God in Christ Jesus our Lord" (Rom 8:38–39). The Blessed Holy Trinity declares the inevitability of our eternal salvation. It is "blessed assurance."

7

Incarnation and Language

ONE OF THE GOALS of the twentieth century movement called Analytic Philosophy was "conceptual clarity." There was nothing particularly new about such a notion, and in seeking that clarity one of its leading proponents, Ludwig Wittgenstein (1889–1951), pointed to the fact that most problems in philosophy were created by confusion in the use of language.[1] A whole field of intellectual inquiry eventually burst forth, often called the Linguistic Turn, or the Philosophy of Language.[2] It has had an exciting history in every respect, and has inadvertently assisted in giving "Religious Language" as much legitimacy as any other linguistic system.

My interest in this is to announce my agreement with the likes of Wittgenstein, albeit with a change in subject matter. Could this non-believing Austrian be any more "on target" when it comes to much in Christian Theology, and particularly to the often vaguely defined Theology of the Incarnation. The first essay here was titled, "My Incarnational Muddle," and I am now declaring that both Christology and Soteriology are each, if anything, a "linguistic muddle."

Christianity burst onto the historic scene with a confused, imprecise vocabulary and language about its most important doctrines, but also about its central figure, Jesus Christ. By about 100 CE its "Scripture" was in place and canonized as the New Testament.

1. Wittgenstein, *Tractatus*, 109.
2. Rorty, *Linguistic Turn*, 1—10.

Early church leaders and Fathers recognized several imprecisions and a confirming lack of clarity, but deemed the verses and pericopes "inspired word" not to be tampered with. Even with respectful acknowledgement and deferential comment, those imprecisions remain these two thousand years later.

In retrospect, it is easy to state that it was quite impossible for the editors and redactors of the twenty-seven books of the New Testament to present an adequate Christian Theology, much less an adequate verbal interpretation of the Person and Work of Jesus Christ. Despite all notions of inspiration in creating sacred texts, the several writers had neither the time nor talent, the wisdom nor insight, to interpret Jesus Christ in any final form, and that for all the ages. If Jesus died approximately 30 CE, and the New Testament was complete by 100 CE, the math shows a mere seventy years for early Christians to reflect on and formalize a Theology of the Incarnation. The Scripture writers and editors had the singular goal to communicate to the world that something uniquely marvelous had happened in their time. The Good News was simply that a Savior had come into a bleak, sad world. Their casualness and looseness in penning texts does not detract from that clear and certain fact. Gratefully, we are left with the texts as we find them, and we deal with them as the divine treasures they are.

Some of the issues of linguistic and conceptual imprecision are easy to demonstrate. I will list a few of them here with very brief commentary.

1. Biblical terms, titles, and names applied to Jesus Christ by himself and by others. The problem is exacerbated by the fact that no guide or recognized standard exists in either Scripture or Christian Theology for dealing with this issue. Thus the believer is always confronted with questions about when to use: "Jesus," "Jesus Christ," "Christ," "the Christ," "Word," "Spirit," "Son of God," "Son of Man," "Messiah," "Savior," et alia. The terms are not self-evidently interchangeable, and improper use may lead to dizzying confusion related to the concurrent Union. Inexactness here can suggest a conflating of the divine and human, or worse, a dyad entity. Perhaps the

most ambiguous, imprecise words in all of Christianity are those most often heard: "Jesus," and "Christ." Do they refer to the human only, the Incarnate Union, the Second Person, the One resurrected, the One at God's right hand? And in what combination?

2. Verbal ambiguities in many sacred texts. Any verse must be carefully considered which confers divine attributes on the "human" Jesus. Likewise, all Scripture must be declared non-literal which states that God the Second Person "became" flesh, was born, or that he died. Many usages of "Christ" are extremely convoluted, and must be examined for these same reasons.

3. Terms and concepts from Jewish Cultic Theology applied to Jesus Christ. The Incarnation was revealed to the world of first century Judaism, and partly because of the ignominious death by crucifixion, was understandably viewed in terms of Cultic vocabulary. Its familiar terms included "atonement," "sacrifice," "substitution," "propitiation," etc. Quite slowly, Christian Theology came to see the limited ability of those concepts to adequately and completely analyze and interpret the larger implications of Incarnation. Though inseparably linked and integrated into the entirety of Judeo-Christian thought, that language must be reimagined and clarified to show where it is thoroughly inadequate or even misleading.

4. Imprecise, muddled language often used in Christian devotion. This fuzziness appears regularly in Christian hymnody, where the focus is almost always on "Jesus, the man." As a child in the American Southern Evangelical tradition, I well remember the heart-tugging songs and hymns which invited an almost embarrassingly too familiar relationship with the Incarnate One. They admonished believers to "have a little talk with Jesus," or to join him for a walk in the Garden alone. They often implied that friendship with Jesus was extremely casual, much like having someone for coffee or an evening meal. None of that is wrong or disrespectful, per se. But believers must recognize that they are not in the presence of "the human, Jesus," but of the Lord God Almighty in Union with

that Jesus of Nazareth. Awe and reverence are the appropriate approaches to the intimacy of this precious and holy relationship. Language used must bear that out always.

5. Ponderous wording of the many Christian Creeds. These priceless documents and expressions of faith do not make light reading. It must be remembered that they were not intended to stand alone, but to be incorporated with other materials and objects used in faith formation and worship. The Creeds are living testimony to the point of this essay: Incarnation presents linguistic challenges which can be addressed and remediated only by a careful, intentional ordering of the words and phrases of faith. Had the texts of Holy Scripture given clear, concise, understandable definitions of Christology, no Creed centering on the Person would have been necessary. The Fathers attended to their tasks painstakingly, constructing linguistic gems which have guided and blessed the church for centuries.

6. Baffling historical labels from early Christological battles. I have humorously addressed my seminary confrontations with terms, names, and concepts from internecine wars over heresy in the young church. Defining and clarifying those ideas and positions is a monumental scholarly undertaking, and has thankfully been done by others. My simple point is to assert that the "alphabet soup" of terms arising in those early days may be thought remote and valueless to modern ears. But important notice must be taken. A few of those theologies, once termed heresy, have in no way disappeared from ecclesiastical thinking. They are, in fact, found to be quite pervasive and influential today. I am convinced that Docetism is a prominent ingredient in current Christological understanding. The notion that Jesus just "seems" to be a man has not left church teaching. Perhaps fewer people advance the Monophysite ideas that Jesus Christ is far more God than man. Nevertheless, that presence is identifiable, undoubtedly. I am convinced that Eutycheanism is an extremely dominant mindset. This is the view that in the Incarnation God and man combine into a new being, a new creature. Adhering to this thinking, it would

be totally incorrect to state that Jesus Christ was fully God and fully man. That language would be useless, even nonsensical, for it would not at all refer to the One who appeared in history. A unique, composite God-man was the being created by the Trinity, and sent to bring salvation.

My goal in this essay is not to clarifyingly resolve these troubling linguistic, and conceptual issues, nor to erect road signs which will lead believers out of the morass. That cannot be done. The situation is, in many instances, hopelessly intractable and quite irremediable. My aim is to call attention to the concerns, point out genuine problems, and to encourage and urge the requisite caution upon all who enter the confusing realms of the Theology of the Incarnation. What solutions there are must be found in how the ideas and concepts are presented and communicated. They must always be Gospel, exceeding "Good News," and not florid verbal display, nor an indecipherable word salad. That is the perennial challenge of those whose desire is to share eternal truth by word, written or spoken.

8

The Captivity of Incarnation

IRONICALLY, THE PRIME INITIATOR of the Protestant Reformation chose not to pen "Systematic Theology." He employed a completely discursive style, in imitation of the Bible, and in particular following the often disjointed writings of the Apostle Paul. Martin Luther's (1483–1564) thought is acknowledged genius, albeit in a severely rambling form. Regardless, it accomplished its bombshell effect, and the Christian Church was never the same thereafter.

Early "Lutheranism" did, however, produce a systematic theologian in Phillip Melancthon (1497–1560). This friend of, and collaborator with, Luther set the stage for much Lutheran-Reformed thought which followed. Unfortunately, many of those later thinkers reverted to an oppressive form of Medieval Scholastic writing, producing tomes seemingly intended for other theologians, certainly not for the average literate believer, or even the typical local pastor.

My interest in Melancthon relates to his oft-quoted, short sentence: We know Christ by his benefits and merits.[1] This is a crucial insight and guiding principle for all studies in the Person and Work of Jesus Christ. Melancthon is asserting that the only way to truly grasp the significance of the "historical Jesus Christ," is to view his life temporally and spiritually. If he is correct, it can be stated categorically that interest in the One who lived and died cannot be separated from the spiritual benefits and merits proffered in that life and death.

---

1. Melancthon, *Loci communes*, 24.

The Captivity of Incarnation

Anyone can write about the human, Jesus, but unless they acknowledge the spiritual aspects and benefits of the Incarnate life, they cannot tell an adequate story. Jesus Christ is not to be studied as a mere mortal man in the same way other men and women are studied and written about. Christian Faith posits that any such telling will be totally and absolutely wrong because decidedly incomplete.

The only persons who understand and affirm this, however, are those for whom Jesus Christ actually offers and brings these benefits and merits. Such believers have been, throughout history, called Christ-followers, Christians. Oddly, in the entire twenty-seven books of the New Testament, the word, Christian, occurs only three times (Acts 11, 26, and 1 Peter 4). To be sure other terms are used for these followers, and regardless of label, all such persons shared a common faith that the Incarnate One changed lives and hearts. They used such idiosyncratic language as "born again," and "saved." They would refer to the Nazarene as "Lord" and "Savior."

Naturally, these believers had been told about this Godly beneficence from the only logical place: Christian fellowship groups and their emerging leaders. This, of course, must be the historical case. I focus on that obvious fact in order to elaborate further on things mentioned in an earlier essay. My critical comment is that as the church developed and expanded, it became more and more constricted in its theological thinking. As it became a greater social and political power, it defined Orthodoxy with an overt exclusionary principle built into its robust theology. So-called and identified "Heretics" were not invited into dialogue, but often branded, ostracized, and excommunicated. The church entered into a very long history of militantly using such practices and methods, marginalizing those whose ideas did not conform. Armed Crusades were employed and celebrated as proper means to bring both suspect believers and non-believers to heel. The church was quite willing to enforce theological unity with both words and swords.

St. Cyprian's famous, "Outside the church there is no salvation!" should have been expanded, for it actually meant, "Outside the church and its self-defined Orthodox Theology there is no salvation!"[2] The church brazenly claimed ownership of the "Keys of the Kingdom," and openly stated that only through its ministrations could one receive the merits and benefits of Jesus Christ. The Kingdom doors were shut to everyone else. Then, in the High Middle Ages, everything changed. An Augustinian monk stepped into history at an electric moment.

In his brashness, Martin Luther bravely but dangerously declared that the Roman Papacy had quite intentionally snared and caged Christianity in its unbiblical theology. With a sharp eye to the Old Testament, he proclaimed that this was the "Babylonian Captivity of the Church."[3] Luther built his entire reforming ministry on this observed premise, and it emboldened the shaping of an alternate way of defining Christianity. The church of Christ had to break the chains of the entrenched Roman Catholicism, and rediscover and reconceptualize itself. A movement began with Luther's aggressive and dramatic protests, now called correctly, Protestantism.

As a member, and an ordained clergy, I am proudly a "child of the church." I gratefully acknowledge that the Institution is an honored caretaker of all things Christian, including the Theology of the Incarnation. It is not the owner of that treasure, however. In these essays I am insisting that ardent believers attack and burst all bonds of any ideology which insularly enslaves and concretizes definitions of Christianity and its capstone doctrine, Incarnation. Only in a radical intellectual and spiritual freedom can it claim its rightful place as the universal, cosmic, saving power of God. The ultimate expression and appropriation of the merits and benefits of Jesus Christ will be the worldwide proclamation that God in Jesus of Nazareth dispenses these gifts outward from the church to all persons. Mercifully, these blessings extend from Creation to Consummation, and then forever!

2. Cyprian, quoted in Ware, *Orthodox Church,* 247.

3. One of three seminal works by Martin Luther in the early Protestant Reformation.

9

Believing Before Breakfast

I HAVE OFTEN THOUGHT that those of us who believe that God was in Jesus of Nazareth, that Incarnation is factual and "real," are in a curious cognitive and intellectual place. We profess our undying devotion to a truth that many nonbelievers may justifiably find strange, unusual, even irrational. The very idea on an all-powerful, all-loving Creator God joining humanity, then manifesting that reality in the life of a living, breathing man in, of all unimportant, back water places as ancient Israel, the wording of our faith claim can instantly produce incredulous looks from our kind, if non-believing, colleagues and friends.

In a playful mood, they may, in fact, describe us as very much like the Queen in *Alice in Wonderland*. She glibly stated to Alice that early in her life she had practiced believing in "impossible things."[1] She said that when she was young, she always did if for half an hour a day, declaring that she sometimes believed as many as six impossible things before breakfast! As humorous as that is, from the remarkable fantasy by Lewis Carroll (1832–1898), the quote can reflect a challenge to believers. Do we, in truth, believe in impossible things? And considering our own individual faith experiences, should we not honestly ask why we believe at all? And what is the actual content of what we find ourselves believing?

1. Carroll, *Alice's Adventures*, 42.

Let us look a little deeper into this important spiritual matter. There are two quite distinct topics for exploration here. They are entirely separable for study purposes, but inseparable for those who understand them as aspects of belief. I refer to 1.) The origin of individual faith, and 2.) The transmission of the content of that faith. I address the last subject here, and the question of origins in the next essay.

As a religion Christianity claims to be founded upon a unique, never to be repeated historical event, the Incarnation. The audience of persons elected to receive and experience this revelation were primarily unlearned first century Jews. Jesus Christ lived and died having spent his earthly time among these, as the Old Testament described them, "chosen people." Those who came to write about his miraculous appearance, some thirty to eighty years later, were, with the exception of Saul of Tarsus, neither philosophers nor theologians. How could believers transmit to others the eternal facts of the world's newest religion?

Naturally, given the historical era, the faith was passed down orally. Writing of texts would come later when the highly circulated oral traditions were finally collected and committed to "paper." The oral sources and written fragments were thereafter creatively knit together by scribes, editors, and redactors to become, in time, the four Gospels. The other twenty-three books of the New Testament were being composed contemporaneously as well. Their subject matter was not exclusively data about the "historical" Jesus Christ, as were the gospels. In fact, the Apostle Paul in all likelihood penned most of his large corpus with little knowledge of the Gospel materials. Knowledge of those accounts among other writers appears sketchy.

Whatever the content of its expanding faith data, it is clear that the faith of early disciples was founded upon what had been "handed down" to them in their respective venues of fellowship, worship, learning, and service. Here, we think of the Greek word, "paradidomi," found in numerous New Testament texts. Its essential meaning is just that: to hand over, to place in another's possession some object, idea, even concept. The Apostle Paul famously uses the term six times. Two are highly instructive here. In 1 Corinthians

11:23, he writes that he "received from the Lord that which I have handed over to you. . . ." He then repeats and reports teaching surrounding the Last Supper, the first Holy Communion. He does not tell how he "received" it, but he claims it came from Jesus Christ.

Then in 1 Corinthians 15:3, he uses the same language for describing faith transmission to these Greek believers. He does not reveal the source of the information that once more was handed to him. It must also be from the Lord, but that is conjecture. The data now delivered is some of the most important in the New Testament and therefore in Christian history: "For I delivered to you as of first importance what I also received, that Christ died . . . and that he was raised to life"(15:3). He goes on to give a list of the reliable witnesses to the Resurrection. For reasons I will speculate about in a later essay, here the Apostle does not mention the very first Easter Morning witnesses, mentioned nonetheless in all four Gospels. He omits the women.

Paul had preached about these truths; now he was writing about them. And that is precisely how the data and content of Christian belief was transmitted in the early era. The Apostle himself had written in Romans (10:17) that faith comes by hearing. Those first auditors were listening to the very words of Scripture before they were ever committed to writing. It must be noted with strong emphasis that soon enough those words of the emergent Holy Writ became a significant part of the data of faith itself. One can make the case that in Protestantism, it became the most important element of faith, as the Bible was equated with the literal words spoken by God. It can be said that many Protestants believe in Father, Son, Holy Spirit, and Bible, perhaps not in that order!

The church has a checkered history when it comes to means and methods of handing the faith to succeeding generations. The practice of educating disciples has included didactic preaching, catechetical instruction, confirmation training, printed literature, and the dramatic, amazing rise of the Sunday School movement. Bible colleges, universities, and seminaries are everywhere to be found, attempting to convey faith and practice to learners in an academic environment. Innumerable Bible societies distribute millions of Scripture texts worldwide, on the assumption that faith comes not only by hearing, but also by reading. The massive enterprise of handing on faith has attempted to be faithful and obedient to Jesus Christ's command to go everywhere making disciples.

But there is a monumentally important caveat to be interjected here. It arises when it is accurately pointed out that the concepts of faith transmission and faith formation presuppose something: individual "faith." Whence its origin? How do we come to believe in the first place? How did this "like precious faith" enter the hearts of believers? Brief comments follow.

10

Believing in Jesus Christ

THERE ARE NO INDEPENDENT sources other than New Testament writings asserting that Jesus of Nazareth actually lived or died. Some references appear in Roman authors and in the writings of Josephus, but those passages are historically suspect. Yet, it would be sorely mistaken to assert that belief in certain people and events must be suspended until a certain kind of "verification" appears. That is a completely flawed methodology, particularly useless in considering Jesus Christ.

Christians claim to know several things about this person: he was indeed a historic figure; he was born, he lived, and he most certainly died. But most crucially, as a historic figure, his life matters eternally, and has everything to do with the believer's life, both here and hereafter. That is affirmed because God was in this Jesus of Nazareth. There is, then, a double-sided aspect to this belief.

This dynamic is demonstrated more than once in the gospels, but perfectly so in the incident at Caesarea Philippi, recorded in Matthew 16:13–28. There, Jesus Christ is accompanied by disciples and he asks a question: "Who do people say I am?" In front of them stands the humanly identifiable historic figure, well known to them. He is not asking if folks around town believe he actually exists as they see him. He is seeking something else. The disciples answer his first query, and momentarily Jesus Christ asks again: "But who do you say I am?" What else is he looking for? As was his undisciplined, impulsive style, the Apostle Peter steps forward and blurts out a remarkable answer: "You are the Christ, the Son of the living God."

As uninhibited as he often was, this time Peter was motivated internally by something beyond his own unfocused impetuosity. This time his answer was divinely inspired and given. Jesus Christ immediately acknowledges Peter's unusual declaration, and ecstatically and joyfully proclaims: You are blessed, Peter, because your newly affirmed faith in me is not of your own doing. You believe in my unique status because Holy God has gifted you with such belief. "Flesh and blood," yours or any other's, did not give you this conviction. It came from "my Father" in heaven. At least one disciple knew, however imperfectly, that God was somehow in Jesus of Nazareth. This Christ had something to do with this world and hopefully the next.

And this is the paradigmatic model for the origin of faith in every believer. The Christian community must relearn this fact in every era, since human pride easily leads to a completely unbiblical attribution in this spiritual discussion. It is too often implied, from pulpit and pen, that faith is acquired quite differently. The believer with total free will must simply open his or her heart, and piously submit to the solicitation offered by the Good Lord. It is the action of the individual alone, so when faith is professed, it becomes a joyous occasion, a meritorious and praiseworthy thing, deserving accolade and congratulations. The sinner has finally "come to Christ." That model is not taught in the New Testament.

It must be carefully noted that the Savior does not applaud Peter for his wise, soul saving decision. Peter had certainly seen a lot of unusual and wonderful things during his travelling days with Jesus of Nazareth. But he did not, nor could he say, that he added all things up and the stunning total compelled him to the only logical explanation: Jesus was the Christ. The Master was perfectly clear: though it is now personally your own, this new faith is a sovereign work of God.

It is an honest question to be asked by all believers: where did my faith originate? Some devout persons report instantaneous awareness of faith, while others trace a longer evolution in coming to a final, firm conviction. I have heard many say something like this: I never remember NOT believing. Churches teaching infant baptism followed by Christian Nurture with Confirmation likely report different examples than those who rely on "crisis conversion" experiences. It must be acknowledged by all, however, that no one should declare that the conviction came after all life facts were analyzed and added up. That smacks of a pure logical deduction and mathematical computation. Drawing a line at the bottom of the page, and reaching an irrefutable, intellectual faith conclusion, must be abandoned as illegitimate in every way.

In some Western Theology, the process and doctrine of how faith occurs is labelled The Election of Grace. God mysteriously chooses who will believe now, and does so for God's own good pleasure. Biblical history and all Christian Theology attest to God's choosing persons, peoples, and nations in order to accomplish and arrange saving events and circumstances for others. It has absolutely nothing to do with eternal "salvation or damnation." Election is a call to serve, pure and simple. It makes great demands and involves both joy and cost, exaltation and suffering. It is, perhaps, an ambiguous blessing!

An important additional ingredient here is the transparently obvious fact that when God gives faith, it does not come with a completely fleshed out theology. The earliest Christians believed without much of anything factually, except having received the gift of belief. Catechetical literature and Creeds came later, as did a text of New Testament Scripture. And the point is easily made that the new followers were not at all in theological unity. The numerous Biblical texts praying and imploring that they all be one, have no divisions, follow only Jesus Christ, affirm one Lord, faith, baptism—they were not written because the church was pristine and pure in theological oneness. Hardly. It has never walked in that kind of lockstep.

That search for unity has gone on unabated since the first Pentecost Sunday. The sometimes on, sometimes off, Ecumenical Movement is testimony to the work of dedicated religious leaders who understand that Christian witness is sorely undermined by the existence of hundreds of denominations and their passionately held systems of belief. Soon after my own ordination I was active in the local work of COCU, the Consultation on Church Union. One soon discovered what was negotiable and what was not among the various denominational representatives. There was much common ground, but the desired Unity was clearly a noble pipedream. To its credit, the international body of the organization did publish a very useful *Common Catechism*, which acknowledged agreements and noted areas for "further study."[1] I needed no reminder, but the proof was there in bold relief: confessing believers in Jesus Christ holding radically different theologies. I did see, however, the beauty of believers demonstrating the goal of the inspirational phrase, "In essentials unity, in non-essentials liberty, in all things charity."[2]

Belief in the divine things of God is forever mysterious and strangely supernal. It is wholly an action of Blessed Holy Trinity, the person contributing nothing to the process. Those coming to believe must thereafter depend on God's ongoing, electing grace in order to attain a more depthful faith, and complete theology, while also participating, as dutiful disciples, in faith transmission to and for others. The Hebrews writer encouraged those who had received faith to move beyond the elementary things of faith (6:1). But in so doing they must never forget that first and foremost came the glorious foundation on which everything stands: God's gift of saving faith in the Lord Jesus Christ.

1. Feiner, *Common Catechism,* chapter one.
2. Beaumont, *Origin of "In Essentials Unity,"* 1.

11

Jesus' Self Awareness

IN OFFERING MY NEW Interpretation of the Incarnation, I have kept constantly in mind the questions asked by Jesus Christ at Caesarea Philippi. He first quizzed disciples: "Who are others saying that I am?" (Mt 16:13). Over many centuries the four answers they gave have been expanded exponentially by students, theologians, and writers to produce additional answers in tomes and volumes now filling shelves in libraries around the world. Many of those writing about this "Son of Man" have also personally and viscerally engaged the second question he asked that fateful day: "But who do you say I am?" (Mt 16:15). As he walked the dusty roads in ancient Israel, who indeed was this person, Jesus Christ, and what was his mission and Work?

There is another question that interjects a new, but indispensable ingredient into any attempt to respond to these two penetrating queries. It is found in the gospel of John, and in the story Jesus Christ is not asking, but is himself being asked a question (Jn 8:51). John first quotes the Lord: ". . . whoever obeys my teaching will never die." The irritated auditors twist the focus and protest that Jesus has a demon because, in point of fact, Father Abraham died, and so did the prophets. Everybody dies. They jeer him asking if he is claiming to be greater than Abraham. Then their abrasive, hostile jab: "Who do you think you are?" (8:53 TEV).

Of course, these demeaning critics were not interested in, nor seeking information for, an answer to the question. They asked only to scorn and deride, convinced that Jesus of Nazareth surely had a demon, and that in addition he had unquestionably blasphemed God by the things he had spoken. They were so incensed and repulsed that they picked up stones to hurl at him, but somehow he secreted himself and got away safely.

The question asked in that hate-filled scenario is troubling enough, but perhaps can be rehabilitated by lifting it out of that indelicate circumstance, and asking it for more acceptable, even devout reasons. Who did this One think he was? What was the content of his self awareness? Whence his self identity? And, did he actually believe he was "part" of an unfathomable Incarnation of God and man?

In pure, free, sovereign grace, the Blessed Holy Trinity chose an unremarkable first century Jewish man with whom to form the Incarnational Union. While there were many Old Testament Scripture texts referring to a divine intervention in the world's affairs, no verse could be cited as a prophetic reference to the one human being, Jesus of Nazareth. Nevertheless, Christian Faith affirms that the Incarnation began with a conception in the womb of Mary of Galilee, and with the male child born thereafter, named Jesus.

Christian Theology can and should freely and boldly inquire into this unique existential and experiential interplay and interaction between God and humanity. In doing so, regrettably, the New Testament helps only minimally, while the formidable Creeds of Chalcedon and Constantinople offer no more than tidbits of tantalizing clues. Is any data accessible and available to aid in our answering? The truth is that there is an almost complete dearth of such data. We must, therefore, speculate. The question is neither impious nor irreverent, but legitimate for Christian Theological inquiry: Was Jesus of Nazareth aware of the Incarnational Union?

The question is pertinent if asked of the Synoptic Gospels; it may be considered scandalously impertinent if asked of the Gospel of John. The latter Gospel is crystal clear that Jesus Christ openly and repeatedly stated such things as he came down from heaven and will return to heaven, that he came from and will return to God (John

6:38; 16:5). The Johannine editors assert categorically that Jesus of Nazareth was aware of the divine-human Union, that he was always none other than fully Jesus Christ. He claims constant revelatory and psychologically supportive contact with his heavenly Father.

John's Gospel is more than problematic here, however, for it can easily be read as if there is, in reality, no human being in the Incarnational Union: there just "seems to be" a human presence in this self-proclaiming "heavenly being." The historical heresy of Docetism taught just such a theology. Docetism is derived from a Greek term meaning "to seem," and can include the ideas of "apparition" and "phantom." Singular focus on John's Gospel always leads the church into this kind of thought. A fully human Jesus of Nazareth can literally "disappear" in much of John's story. Therefore, the Gospel must be balanced by, and where necessary corrected by, comparison and contrast with the Synoptics. Even then, the Jesus Christ presented by John can hardly be harmonized or reconciled with his portrayal in Matthew, Mark, and Luke.

It might appear self-evident that one who could perform mighty acts and wonders would assume a special relationship with a Higher Power. But that is not at all the case. History is replete with instances of "miracle workers" who made no claim to Incarnation as the source of their giftedness. As early as Moses confronting Egyptian magicians, it is both Old and New Testament testimony that strange, frightening, or wonderful things could seemingly be done by persons without an attribution of any divine-human Union. Christian history shares innumerable stories of holy saints raising the dead, curing blindness, and other sundry ailments, all to the glory of God. If, then, our question cannot be answered by reference to the more dramatic, showy, expressive examples of both power and compassion, what data counts?

I personally believe that any satisfactory answer turns on the notion of "will." The Creeds taught what the Gospels only vaguely referenced: there is one Personal Presence and one Personal Identity, but there are two wills. The human will is divinized by the divine, and that "for the salvation of the human race." Without a subservient human will, no sinless life could have been possible. But is there evidence that even this reality was a self-conscious awareness of Jesus of Nazareth? He did say, "Not my will but Thine be done." But those kind of verses are not confirmatory of anything much, since many serious believers use such language, professing in those words their desire to be completely obedient to God.

In the end it appears that Christian Theology has not enough data to access Jesus' internal "frame of mind." We cannot report whether he was aware of the Incarnational Union. The question intrigues, and should be seriously considered in order to determine the implications from any answer given. The inquiry deserves appropriate consideration as part of an all-compassing Theology of the Incarnation. Regardless of that answer, Theology can certainly "move on," and speculate creatively about other important facts, such as the origin of his special gifts, talents, and powers. To those topics we turn in coming essays.

12

Jesus' Self Identity and Scripture

AT HIS BAPTISM BY John, Jesus reportedly heard, "You are my beloved Son!" (Mark 1:11). He interpreted this as a revelatory announcement from God, and the event can correctly be cited as the beginning of the itinerant and deliberate public ministry. From baptism to death on the Cross, Jesus embraced the goal of becoming not only the Son of God, but the Perfect Son of God. Anyone hearing such a heavenly affirmation would have no higher goal than to please the One pronouncing the startling blessing. Jesus would accomplish this remarkable, unique perfection, dying sinless on Golgotha, observed by both sympathetic and hostile onlookers. The inquiry here is this: how did Jesus of Nazareth, in the divine Union, come to understand and define his personal role and place in the first century Jewish religious environment? Where did he derive a self identity to inform his ministry? How did it occur?

Many things can be learned about this dimension of Jesus' self awareness. It has been noted that whether he did or did not grasp the existential Incarnational presence, he demonstrated abilities quite unlike those of any man, certainly any ordinary first century Jew. Many of these self presentations relate to his brilliant interpretive understanding of Old Testament Scripture. A great deal, but not all, of his self identity is transparently derived from these ancient texts. We can discern these themes in selected sayings-deeds, even as we reaffirm this cardinal point: God the Second Person revealed to him and endowed him with the essential features of his self awareness, his powerful gifts, and his spiritual teaching. They were not "naturally" his by virtue of total life experiences. (See next essays for further suggestive approaches to these topics and ideas.)

There is little doubt that the entire ministry of Jesus Christ after the baptism was forged in his thorough immersion in the Scriptures of Israel. He was a diligent student of those writings, but his study took an unusual twist: he personalized pertinent texts as self referential. They were not only speaking to him, but literally defining his personality, his ministry, and his total self identity. They were giving him the evolving, unalterable script for the living of his everyday life. This maturational process included his participation in the teaching ministries of synagogue and Temple, but Christian Faith affirms that the coordinating agent was clearly the Second Person of the Trinity. And, thus, with divine tutoring, at approximately thirty years of age, he was ready to step into history, and to change it forever.

This case can be made with great specificity. The Old Testament is a large volume, hundreds of pages, many themes, topics, and subjects. Why does Jesus of Nazareth focus very selectively on certain texts and not on others, in order to understand and fulfill his God-given mission? Why does he appear to be "claimed" by a specific set of verses and pericopes, which he then "lives out" to his life's tragic end? And the answer is: he is internally led and instructed so to do, and that by the Son of God in the Son of Man.

A fundamental initial understanding was this: Jesus of Nazareth knew existentially, and with sorrow, that God had called corporate Israel to accomplish many things. But the Chosen People had failed, and dramatically. Jesus came to understand himself as the "New Israel"—in one person—who would perfectly live out God's plan to be the light of the world, to open the floodgates of grace and blessing for all. This was not a new mandate, but had been known to all Jews as the fundamental activity of the entire Nation of Israel, after it had settled the "Land of Milk and Honey" (Exod 3:8). Empowered by the Second Person, Jesus of Nazareth believed he would do what had not hitherto been done: the Kingdom of God would come to dispense this eternal, loving mercy through his radical, sweeping new initiative.

Jesus knew well that such a life would involve great personal struggle and suffering. Who among the Chosen would welcome his self-appointed role, and who believe it was authorized by God? None. He would be rejected by his own beloved people. He surely recalled that the Patriarch Jacob had to wrestle with God to receive the name, "Israel"(Gen 32). To accomplish his lofty goals, Jesus would have to likewise struggle, with both peers in the world, and even with the Almighty. In fact, the battles began immediately, for the next steps after his heavenly-affirming baptism took him alone to the Wilderness, compelled there by the very God who had moments before "baptized" him as the Beloved Son (Luke 4:1). His ready knowledge of Old Testament texts aided him in resisting the Tempter there, but at the end of the trial, Luke records ominously, that the tempting One went away only to return at an "opportune time"(4:13). Such "times" would be many, culminating in the plaintive and agonizing cries from the Cross.

If Jesus appropriated concepts and ideas, he also appropriated names and titles from Israel's Scripture. Though the terms are capable of being understood and interpreted in the plural, he applies them to himself, using the first person singular pronoun, "I." Two terms are especially expressive of this: "Son of Man," and "Suffering Servant." What is the Old Testament origin of these titles, and how does Jesus intend them personally?

Son of Man texts appear in the Psalms, Ezekiel, Isaiah, and Daniel. They are highly varied in meaning, but generally refer to a creature of lowly status being exalted by God. This is the usage most often intended by Jesus. The suggestion is that Jesus views himself as THE representative Son of Man, THE HUMAN BEING standing before God for all humanity, all other persons. Jesus seems also convinced that through a coming, mysterious exaltation by God, though ill defined, obscure, and after his death, all human creatures will be blessed through him, THE ONE FOR ALL.

There is admittedly a vagueness in this self definition and the term falls strangely on modern ears. Even so, Son of Man was a common Aramaic locution appropriated by Jesus of Nazareth through the inner prompting of the Second Person. The self deprecation it implied fit Jesus perfectly, since the implication was patently clear that the lowly Son of Man could attain no status at all without an action wholly of God. He had no personal goodness nor could he accomplish anything of righteous merit apart from the presence and power of the Creator. "Why call me good?. . . Only God is good" (Matt 19:17).

Some have maintained that Son of Man contains Messianic overtones, but that issue is a secondary academic one. I do not ascribe such notions to the term since my understanding of Messiahship precludes it at the outset. I will visit that theme in another essay.

While Jesus repeatedly referred to himself as Son of Man, he did not self designate with, "I am the Suffering Servant." Such a proclamation would have been socially off-putting, a profanation, and could only bring disapprobation. He did, however, refer to himself as Servant, and constantly pointed, directly and indirectly, to his own suffering. In this, the ideas coalesce. There is no doubt that his self interpretations here came from the Servant Poems of Deutero-Isaiah. Therein, the themes are diverse and complicated, referring both to individual personages and to a corporate entity. Jesus could identify with both, as we have seen. But ominously, the ancient texts openly declare that the Servant will be stricken and smitten, literally brought to great suffering, by the very Lord God of the Servant himself. Jesus of Nazareth does not shy away from this self imposed and painful destiny. Rather, guided and consoled by the inner, mysterious influence of the Incarnate Union, he bravely embraces it, all the way to death by execution. His God is on that hill of death, also.

Jesus accepts and utilizes the titles of Beloved Son of God, Son of Man, and Servant who suffers. There are other titles which need attention, including Messiah.

13

How God Experiences and Influences Jesus

THE CREED OF CHALCEDON gives an historic, detailed, and theologically invaluable definition of the Person of Jesus Christ. It does not indicate how God, the Second Person of the Trinity, actually influences Jesus of Nazareth to ensure that he remains faithful until his death. The writings of the New Testament are silent on this subject, as is Christian Theology. This is evidence enough to raise every caution in attempting to describe this influence. The action and process of the Son of God teaching, guiding, protecting, and empowering Jesus, leading him to overcome every temptation, is clearly beyond our cognitive ken. We cannot know. However, in just such matters believers may speculate and offer suggestions appropriate to the spiritual seriousness of the topic. I will here offer some thoughts in that devotional vein.

In faithful, honest Christian Theological endeavors, no one should claim to know things not known, nor to assert things to be the case without any supporting data to "back up" such claims. Fideism is the position which maintains that one can indeed have "faith" independent of reason or without what might be termed proofs for a claim or position. Faith and reason are here juxtaposed as opposites, with even such a genius as the philosopher, Immanuel Kant (1724–1804), stating that reason must be discarded to make room for faith.[1] While that is a radical, wrong-headed formulation of the issue, no one should go in the opposite direction by affirming that faith is built on, or the result of, reason. The faith-reason dialogue will forever be somewhere in the ether of theological and philosophical discussion, continuing to create unnecessary confusion.

In the Foundational Principles for the Theology of the Incarnation, I made assertions that the Second Person of the Trinity experiences the total life of Jesus of Nazareth. What are evidences for such claims? I also wrote in those Foundations that the intrapersonal interaction between God and man is admittedly a nearly opaque subject, with only allusions in Creed and Holy Writ to enable believers to speak about it. On the other hand, Christian Theology has been given, in selected Synoptic passages, and highlighted in the Creed of Chalcedon, ideas which may after all help in this inquiry. Both describe a Perfect Union, one with differentiating properties and two distinct wills. The observation that Faith can identify some of these differences, while simultaneously professing the inseparable Union, may provide a useful, if limited, understanding of the dynamic relationship between God the Son and Jesus of Nazareth.

I will suggest two approaches which can assist believers to better understand the relationship. First, I propose a paradigm sentence which can provide an entre for further reflection. I will purposely exaggerate the wording to illustrate where the concept might lead: WHEN JESUS OF NAZARETH EXPERIENCES (X), THE SECOND PERSON OF THE HOLY TRINITY EXPERIENCES JESUS' EXPERIENCE, BUT AS INFINITE GOD DOES NOT "LIVE" THE IDENTICAL, FINITE, HUMAN EXPERIENCE OF JESUS.

A simple, less wordy example demonstrates the point of this approach: "When Jesus experiences hunger, the Second Person engages, undergoes, and indwells Jesus' experience of hunger, but is not thereby hungry." The model sentence can be used to describe every psychological, physical, intellectual, spiritual, and emotional experience of Jesus. It can present a reasonable linguistic and cognitive model for understanding the human-divine interaction. While it is functionally descriptive, it can include everyone of Jesus' life

---

1. Seddon, "*Kant on Faith*," 189.

experiences: birth, temptation, frustration, rage, alienation, thirst, et al. Of course, its usefulness terminates with the last possible example: "When Jesus of Nazareth dies on the Cross, the Second Person compassionately and empathically experiences Jesus' experience, but as God does not thereby die."

The model's basic wording serves to both preserve the Union and also to recognize the differentiating properties. It creates a heuristic method and process for the important affirmation: the Second Person experiences the entire human life of Jesus of Nazareth.

If this approach has merit, it may well assist in understanding the other, perhaps "opposite" aspect of the subject: how the Second Person influences Jesus of Nazareth. If it can be established that God experiences the life of Jesus, it is reasonable to assert that that experience is precisely the point of contact, the portal, for the divine empowerment, which may include signs and wonders. Just there, God the Son inwardly guides, directs, nurtures, comforts, corrects, and teaches Jesus, in every human act. Thus, it can be acknowledged, as the Foundation principle states: the sinless life is not the autonomous achievement of Jesus of Nazareth. It is the miraculous inwardness of the Incarnate Union.

As a concluding aside, Christian Faith and Scripture have always maintained that believers "possess" the Holy Spirit. Yet, this is another example of very muddled language, for the thing possessed may be variously labelled, "the Holy Spirit," "the Spirit of Christ," "Jesus Christ," or even "God." It appears that the various texts of reference share a common message, that in the inner person a divine presence critiques impure thoughts, motives, and actions, while encouraging and directly aiding the believer in every holy endeavor. In any event, a full understanding of what this actually means for ordinary humans ends in a "glass darkly," a mysterious uncertainty. Despite that apparent fact, the language of Scripture may offer helpful and suggestive ideas for a framework of discussion. The qualitative and quantitative difference between what happens in the Incarnation, and in the life of all other persons, is glaringly obvious. But it does seem that the Lord God Almighty deigns to influence and affect sinful humanity in ways very similar to the divine work in the Incarnate Union.

14

Sinless? How?

ATTENTIVE READERS OF THE Foundational Principles for the Theology of the Incarnation, and the previous few essays, will know immediately how I intend to answer the question of this essay. Principle number forty-seven affirms that the sinless perfection of Jesus of Nazareth was in no sense his own autonomous achievement, but was inwardly facilitated by the mysterious working of the Second Person. Through the Incarnate Union, Jesus was able to live and to die sinless. In order to accomplish this, he needed "help." If that is the "short answer," there are nevertheless several aspects of this issue which demand attention.

In text and teaching, Christian Faith has always maintained that Jesus of Nazareth dies sinless on Good Friday. It takes no scholarly profundity to ask, "Just how was this possible? How did Jesus overcome every temptation to sin?" It is completely fatuous for scoffers to cast the aspersion that in the thirty years of Jesus' physical and psycho-sexual development he must certainly have broken the laws of God. That is a comment which rests on the correct assumption that, "Everybody sins!" But in Christian Faith and Theology, that is precisely the point. The claim is large and sweeping, but believers are confident in proclaiming what is Scripturally taught, that Jesus of Nazareth as Jesus Christ did not sin.

The church simply stipulates this claim, with no interest in entering a fruitless argument or debate. It is a statement of faith, a credo, and it rests not on belief in Jesus' human power and ability, but on belief in the power of God in the divine Union. Christians are beyond sure that as a man, Jesus of Nazareth could not so live, but equally sure that in the Incarnation, miraculously, he did.

The bold assertion that he was sinless due to the divine Concurrence suggests that he could, in fact, have sinned. Was Jesus peccable, capable of sin? If the answer were, "No!," then the whole discussion would be a fraudulent sham, and affirming his sinlessness a quite meaningless ruse. The Hebrews writer gives the classic verse for this inquiry. In that book he writes that Jesus was tempted in all the ways everyone is tempted, yet without sin. Had he been unable to sin, the verse, and much of the Book of Hebrews, would be a fantastic, self-serving irrelevance. So would most of the New Testament.

To ask if Jesus could sin introduces another concern. What is the standard by which he would be judged to have sinned? And this is a matter demanding considered reflection. If a modern or ancient person quizzed Jewish religious leaders of the first century, they would say in tandem that Jesus had broken and violated many of the laws of God. They would have no qualms in labelling him a profligate, deliberate, blasphemer—a rank sinner. That they did so identify him is highlighted multiple times in all four Gospels. They were insulted by his insolent disregard for the teachings about lifestyle matters on which they alone could pontificate. The tense interaction between Jesus and the Pharisees, in particular, often revolved around the issue: "Who gave you the right or authority to do or say this or that?" Those leaders viewed him as a mere man, therefore a guilty usurper. They had a long history of dealing violently with such crass offenders. Stoning or crucifixion under Roman jurisprudence, suited nicely. Humanly speaking, their chagrin is easily understandable, but in Christian historical retrospect, is viewed less charitably. However, any perpetuation of the notion of "Jewish guilt" for Jesus' death is profoundly misguided and theologically irrelevant.

The concept of "authority" introduces a second topic integral to Incarnational Theology. Its definition is a critical one in grasping God's influence in the Concurrent Union. The term literally means that some sort of power is conferred, handed to, or passed on to a recipient. Authority is not inherent, but is an endowment. The human Jesus is so endowed with that power by the Second Person, and by virtue of that self understanding, he does and says many radical, counter-cultural things. Through the Union, he is fearlessly emboldened to "cross swords" with the high and the mighty. He avowed that he had come "to fulfill the law," and was therefore guilty of no wrongdoing regarding it. Harsh criticism of humanly-created "traditions" was another matter, however. That he did in "righteous indignation."

With the few Biblical texts available, it can be rightly concluded that Christian Faith cannot pronounce with absolute, smug certainty upon the content of the recurring divine, spiritual influence that allowed Jesus of Nazareth to resist the numberless temptations that came his way. Believers resort to the position that his life drama is the stuff of miracle, mystery, and Godly action beyond our knowing. Christians can, however, offer evidence from their own discipleship, thus providing a helpful analogous comparison between the Incarnate life and that of ordinary followers. How does God influence and inform Christians, offering grace to resist sin and to stay the spiritual course?

The answers and terms here are known to all believers and familiar enough, even as it acknowledged that they must be applied in unique ways to the Incarnate One. They are old words of faith: grace, mercy, nurture, presence, care, love, providence. Jesus of Nazareth comes to know and experience these gifts in extraordinary ways. Appropriately, his life was perpetually filled with gratitude and thanksgiving. So must every believer respond to God's loving largesse for these special, heavenly bestowals.

Christian Faith cannot anatomatize nor minutely describe the dynamic process of Jesus' sinless living. But the Apostle Paul, in 1 Corinthians 10:13, penned a perfect verse for consideration here: "There hath no temptation taken you but such as is common to all: but God is faithful and will with the temptation make a way of escape, that you may be able to bear it" (KJV). The verse speaks confidently to what God does for ordinary believers in times of trial. But if applied to Jesus of Nazareth, it would clearly read that the "way of escape," that is, the power to overcome and resist, was always and solely the divine influencing presence of the Second Person of the Trinity.

The sinlessness of Jesus is Christianity's diamond concept, which has many facets, to continue the comparison. The Faith is not concerned with whether Jesus was "a good man," or "a great teacher." There have, gratefully, been scores of such persons throughout history. But these qualities and characteristics hardly indicate that such leaders open an avenue directly to God. Usually, they claim no such status as Incarnate Son of God.

Sinlessness can be misapplied, however, when it is attached to some Jewish Cultic notions such as substitution and sacrifice. Bulls and goats were never perfect sacrifices, but always blemished in some way. Jesus as sinless is unqualifiedly unblemished, therefore the perfect substitutionary "sacrifice." This long-standing teaching of a large segment of Christianity is integral to a certain brand of theology. The shorthand version is this: humans have sinned, are enslaved and imprisoned by sin, and an offended God rightly demands "justice." Jesus is perfect, dies sinless, God's anger is assuaged, and sinners can claim an eternal heaven if only they will "accept" the grace and forgiveness proffered in Jesus' death. Jesus dies as a substitute for the rightfully-deserved eternal death of all sinners. God does the accounting, and individuals can quite easily move from the category of "lost" to that of "saved." To aid in this computational process, there is a "Book of Life" (Rev 20:15) in which God inscribes the names of those who have accepted Jesus, and are on their heavenward way.

I have argued that this theology downplays the requirement for human perfection, that it short circuits and undermines the entire drama of human persons going from life on earth to life in the Kingdom which has no end. It portrays God's action as "magically" transforming sinners to saints, with no necessity that they rid themselves of every vestige of sin. In this theology, God's forgiveness of sins is equated with total internal and eternal transformation, quite enough to allow God to open heaven to these forgiven ones.

Forgiveness is not enough. Elsewhere I have stated that it is "the divine incompletion." It is the essential first step, and must accompany all persons on the arduous path to perfect holiness. Forgiveness, by itself, however, cannot produce this perfection.

Any theology of substitutionary atonement has the very unfortunate effect of declaring that Jesus achieved perfect holiness so that all other persons do not have to do so. That is a completely erroneous, and wholly unsatisfactory, understanding and interpretation of Christianity.

15

When the Messiah?

THE QUESTION OF WHETHER Jesus self referred as Messiah is not an inquiry to be made of the Gospel of John. There Jesus openly and repeatedly tells many individuals and groups of people that he is, indeed, "Messiah." Perhaps the best verse exemplifying this trend in that gospel is 18:20–21. There, before the High Priest, Jesus speaks these revealing words: "I have always spoken publicly to everyone; I have never said anything in secret." This statement perfectly matches John's unquestioned certainty that Jesus boldly characterized his own status and standing as completely and totally bestowed by God. He and God were in constant and intimate contact and communication. It can be maintained that because of these numerous declarations, the "human" Jesus of Nazareth is almost completely overshadowed and subsumed by a novel divine being and entity.

These passages abound from the Johannine editors. They are convinced that, however defined, Jesus was wholly, transparently, and continuously infused with divine power and presence. I maintain that precisely because of this, Jesus, the Messiah of John's Gospel, is not peccable, but totally incapable of violating God's law in any way whatsoever. To ask if such a being could sin would be unthinkable. There is here no divinized human will, only a divine will. Thus, there is no "conflict" of wills, as in "not my will but Thine be done" (Luke 22:42). And there is no agony in the Garden of

Gethsemane, no "My God, my God, why have you forsaken me!" (Matt 27:46). from John's rather stoic victim of crucifixion.

In John's Gospel there are nearly fifty verses in which Jesus affirms his divine, even supernatural identity. Statistically, this is a highly significant "cohort" which cannot be dismissed when compared to what appears in the Synoptics. No one can imagine the Jesus Christ of the Synoptics pronouncing about himself in the way he does in the Gospel of John. The portrayals are incommensurate, even contradictory.

For over one hundred years, more liberal Biblical scholars have referenced the "Messianic Secret," that Jesus stated emphatically, and on multiple occasions, "Do not tell anyone!"[1] These implorations followed acts and words which had led disciples and others touched by his deeds, to make declarations about his manifestly unique, even otherworldly status. In the Synoptics, Jesus appears discreet, not at all desirous of being publicly identified with the highly-charged label, "Messiah."

Many verses can be presented which demonstrate Jesus' desire for something like secrecy in this matter: Mark 1:43–45, 3:12, 5:43, 8:29–30, 9:9. If Mark was the primary source for Matthew and Luke, Jesus' words in Mt 16:20, and Luke 8:56, 9:21 match the concept. But the most telling fact remains that there is no verse in the Synoptics in which Jesus affirms, "I am the Messiah." The text in Mark 14:62 has an earlier variant, likely the oldest, in which Jesus does not say , "I am the Christ," but the more logically correct, "You say that I am."

The verse in question here comes from the sham trial before his crucifixion, wherein the High Priest asks, "Art thou the Christ?" The indirect answer, "You are saying so. . . . ," is perfectly in line with many responses to such questioning throughout his ministry, and especially at these legal proceedings. (Luke 22:70; Matt 27:11; Mark 15:2). It seems completely improbable that Jesus Christ would reveal his true identity only at this point in his life, and in front of such treacherous people who had no interest whatsoever in his credentials, divine or otherwise. Jesus Christ knew he was already a

---

1. Wrede, *Messianic Secret*. The entire work devoted to demonstrating his position.

"dead man," convicted long before the rigged hearings. The several audiences before whom he appeared had one goal only. . . to be permanently rid of him and his teaching. His addressing Messiahship was a complete irrelevancy to the trial outcome.

He has come to be called that since the first days of the Christian movement, so why would Jesus Christ not want everyone to confess that he is God's long-awaited Messiah? Why the Messianic Secret? The meaning and interpretation of this Messianic Secret is not self-evidently clear, and is subject to several responses and answers. Here, I will list a few of them, adding my comments before offering my own position at the conclusion.

> One: Jesus Christ's understanding of Messiah was very different from that of the Jewish leadership or populace. He will not trade on this confusing, problematic term. He knew that in the Old Testament, ideas and concepts about Messiah varied greatly. The most appealing notion among his contemporaries, the Roman-oppressed Jews of Palestine, would naturally be a Messiah "armed and dangerous," capable of ridding the Promised Land of the army of occupation and suppression. First century demoralized Jews could not be expected to embrace another Old Testament image as the agent of change, a leader who would rely on moral teaching, and even meekly go to the "slaughterer dumb" (Isaiah 53:7). They sought a forceful military-politician, not a passive devotee. Relief from their servant status required power, not moral suasion. It is quite noteworthy that in whatever way Jesus Christ lived out his life, he often ran headlong into conflict with Jewish leaders, and often over ideas about Messiahship. That tension often reached a veritable boiling point.

> Two: Any revelation of Messiahship in his lifetime, in his socioreligious context, would confine the entire idea and concept of Incarnate Messiah to Jewish interpretations only. It would ensure a complete, total interpretive absorption in the the Cultic Theology of Israel. The Second Person, not Jesus of Nazareth, must prevent this in order to universalize its significance by freeing it from an inseparable attachment to Old

Testament concepts. Messiah as a term has status by reference to distinctively Old Testament ideas. Incarnation does not.

Three: If Jesus of Nazareth was totally unaware of the Union in Incarnation, he would have vehemently rejected such self-referential language as inappropriately arrogating to himself the lofty spiritual title. It would have been sinful blasphemy. He was, after all, a good Jew who knew the Scriptures.

Four: There is the idea that Jesus Christ did not claim Messiahship for fear of premature arrest. This view turns on his having a calculated timetable for the completion of his divine mission, and that he well foreknew his demise would eventuate in death. This view minimalizes what appears to be the great spontaneity in his life, in exchange for a rigidity based upon his ability to foretell future outcomes. These assumptions cannot be demonstrated Biblically, making the conclusions implausible. It cannot be determined that when he was arrested, Jesus Christ was completely satisfied that he had accomplished his divine goals. Rather, the ending points to great incompletion as a very young man dies criminally.

Five: My interpretation can be stated simply: Messiahship was not a divinely endowed lifelong title, but one which could only be bestowed at the end of the perfect, holy, sinless life. It could be received only when the "Beloved Son" of the baptism became the "Perfect Son" of the Cross. Messiah literally means, "one who brings God's salvation." That salvation came at three PM on Good Friday, and not before. The merit of this position is that it makes logical sense in explaining the Messianic Secret of the Synoptics. Jesus Christ's insistence that the disciples "tell no one," is understandable if Messiahship results from life culmination, not from an inherent characteristic and possession. The words from John 19:30 are applicable: "It is finished." They refer to much more than that his life has reached its physical conclusion. As his life ends, a Messiahship begins. God's salvation is now abroad in the world. The Kingdom has come at last!

Rightly so, the early church subordinated the term Messiah to the Greek-derived "Christ." The church was called Christian, and historically not solely identified thereafter by things Jewish. As its own Scripture was produced, it also relied less comprehensively on Old Testament teachings, acknowledging always, however, that Jesus Christ's self understanding was largely a derivative of his reading those Hebrew texts. The environment of his life was Jewish, even as his mission transcended it completely.

16

How Jewish Was the Incarnation?

THIS ESSAY BEGINS WITH a statement and a question. Jesus of Nazareth was a Jew; the Second Person of the Trinity was not. Why has Christianity enchained its Incarnational Theology in Old Testament Jewish Cultic Theology, and perpetuated this highly limiting context for nearly two thousand years now? This has hindered Christianity from accomplishing God's larger intention and mission for Incarnation: the proclamation of universal salvation in and through the emerging Kingdom of God. This essay offers suggestions and ideas for addressing and ameliorating this reality and circumstance.

I continue to affirm that the Blessed Holy Trinity did not intend for the Incarnation to be understood and interpreted by Old Testament Jewish Cultic Theology. Its ritual terms and ideas are familiar enough: substitution, atonement, vicariousness, and sacrifice. There is a strong emphasis on blood and death. Each of its terms must be redefined and reinterpreted.

The Incarnation is, by definition, God's action in Jesus of Nazareth. It is not the reverse: the action of Jesus of Nazareth interfacing with God. The backdrop of the Incarnation is an entire Jewish theological system, as it evolved into the first century, culminating in the collected thirty-nine books of the Old Testament. That theology, like all others historically, contains two essential aspects. One speaks to its understanding of God, nature, and humanity. The other addresses ritual and ceremonial, designed to facilitate worship of

God, and through which God in turn blesses the people. Christianity made the crucial mistake of interpreting Incarnational Theology through the latter, the ritual and ceremony. It wisely kept the Hebraic understanding of God, nature, and humanity, but needlessly appended to it terms, concepts, and ideas related to Cultic practice.

Early Christians, and those who wrote the New Testament, had witnessed, or been told, about the amazing Incarnate One. Though they were not all Jews, they nevertheless rushed to Old Testament texts to discover prophetic teachings by which to contextualize this life. Later Christian theologians uncritically accepted their conclusions and took for granted the perfect applicability of those texts, concepts, and terminology.

Through the Concurrent Union, the Second Person had experienced Jesus' fidelity to that Jewish faith while delicately leading him far beyond its bounds. So in the four Gospels, Jesus does not completely embrace or wholly confine himself to Old Testament ideas alone. His mission and ministry present a larger vision which includes, but radically transcends, anything in his contemporary Jewish ideology. He witnesses to an all-inclusive love for all persons, even the outcasts and "Gentile sinners." This was revolutionary and distasteful to Jewish minds. Today, we might say he broke down barriers of caste and class. Here, he followed the often dismissed Old Testament teaching of God's abiding love for all peoples and all nations. His peculiar self awareness was attributable only to a giftedness from the Union. He bravely spent most of his days at loggerheads with the staid religious leaders due to how he presented the heart of his God.

Christian thinkers after the death on the Cross reflexively seized Old Testament pericopes, sometimes straining to overlay them on facts becoming known or believed about the Person and Work of Jesus Christ. When they were considering and reflecting upon his ignominious crucifixion, they were insistent that principal Jewish Cultic teachings—atonement, substitution, and sacrifice—matched and defined the mysterious, shocking event. With that paradigm firmly ensconced, the focus came to rest squarely on blood and death, the integral notions from Cultic thought. Early Christian Theology continued to find them absolutely applicable in every respect. Consequently, the Old Testament terms were appropriated as the core and central ideas of Christianity. They were essentially "baptized with Christian water."

History has demonstrated their resilience in continuing to inform the theological conversations regarding the Incarnation. That method and approach has left an indelible imprint on all future Christian thought; it has been an immovable object. But in actuality, Old Testament Cultic ideas could never contain, nor provide an adequate framework for, the universal content of the Theology of the Incarnation.

It is ironic that Christianity was ever seen as a religion of atonement, sacrifice, or propitiation, since God's word to the Jews was consistent, powerful, and vigorous: "I take no pleasure in the death of ceremonially slaughtered animals" (Is 1:11; Ps 51:16; Ps 50:8; et al). God was clear enough that probity of life, not animal deaths through the performance of bloody Priestly rituals, was the divine concern. (Micah 6:8; Ps 51:16–17; et al). Nevertheless, Christian emphasis went straight to the Cross, and to the death of Jesus of Nazareth articulated in Jewish terminology. "Jesus was born to die!" could be the high and waving banner of much of Christian Theology for the last two thousand years. With such a microscopic scrutiny of his death, there was an accompanying and unfortunate casualty—a proper focus on his LIFE.

Furthermore, the overweening preoccupation with the "blood of Jesus" needed a constant historical review in face of the fact that crucifixion was not an especially bloody form of execution. Flogging by Roman soldiers could very well be quite grisly, and actually take the victim's life before the formal execution. But the many Biblical and later emotionally charged references to a "fountain filled with blood" should be reexamined for literal historical accuracy.

Atonement, sacrifice, propitiation, et al, are terms indicative of a "legal fiction"— something is declared to be the case when in actuality it is otherwise or not at all. This was profoundly recognized by Old Testament saints, who were ancients, but not naïve. They knew sins were not truly forgiven, but, for lack of better words, "rolled forward" awaiting further saving action from God. Thus the multiple texts acknowledging the artificiality of the practical "forgiveness" in the ritual sacrificial system. Understanding the ineffectiveness of those ritual practices, Christianity appropriated the terms, but confidently proclaimed and preached that Jesus Christ was now the solution to the dilemma, for he was the "perfect sacrifice and atonement for sins." But nothing changed in the fundamental equation. God declared forgiveness, but now through a magical, mystical death on a Cross. By definition, the "new" theology perpetuated the indispensability of Old Testament ideas in the novel religion of Christianity. Jesus Christ simply replaced the menagerie of goats and bulls and doves.

Despite the oft-repeated commands to "Be ye holy as I am holy," Judaism, and much of Christianity, did not properly conceive of the fact that God would save the world, not through a "bloody sacrifice," but through an Incarnate One living a completely perfect, holy life. Nor has either religion been comfortable and convinced that God actuality commands similar perfection from every one of God's beloved children. The death on the Cross transforms no one inwardly, nor does it perform instant perfection in any person. God's forgiveness is immeasurable, but, as I have previously said, it is an incompletion which cannot create perfection.

The relationship between the Old Testament and the Incarnation must be sought in the implications derived from the truth in Foundation Principle number twenty-three: The God of the Incarnation is the same God revealed in the signal events of the Old Testament. My intentional run-on sentence completes my thinking on this issue: the idea of God in a human being allowing the death of the human being in order that the death becomes a substitute, atonement, propitiation, or sacrifice, before the very same God who was Incarnate in the human being, and by this produces an eternal change in God's view of humanity— this is not Christian Theology.

17

Temptation and Holy Perfection

IF THE THEOLOGICAL POINT is registered that God alone saves, and does so by God's own word-deed, all mechanistic, magical, and legally fictitious notions of redemption are to be rejected and abandoned. Any doctrine of Soteriology which declares that God has set up mechanisms and systems and saves persons through some "transaction" within them is purely unbiblical. God saves through an unmediated, direct, personal relationship with each believer-sinner, assuring the individual that upon achieving perfect holiness God will announce, "Well done, good and faithful servant" (Matt 25:21,23).

But how do mere mortals become perfect and holy while maintaining free will in the uniqueness of each personhood? Jesus of Nazareth did so through the sustaining and restraining influence of the Second Person, empowering him to defeat and overcome every temptation. God is our Creator who well understands humanity's need for divine assistance in this process, and lovingly provides grace and mercy, now and throughout eternity, as believers mature into God's well-pleasing children. But we do sin. We will sin. We have sinned. Sin is ever before us (Ps 51:3). In an earlier essay I reviewed the ways God dispensed this grace-filled assistance to Jesus of Nazareth, and by analogy, to us. Now we refocus on the concept of temptation as the vital notion and spiritual reality which leads us to sin. Sadly, Christians recognize that we succumb to temptation, large and small, and continuously. What are the most seductive temptations which lead us astray? Let us inquire into this troublesome area of every human life, lived before a thrice-holy God.

The New Testament Greek word for temptation is "peirasmos," and it refers to things both inward and outward which entice and lead to sin. It is a weighty concept in the text, noticeably used to describe the strenuous kinds struggles Jesus experienced in that remote Wilderness. Human battles with temptations vary from engagements with trivial seductions to greater issues involving persons and nations. Believers must not downplay the idea, but acknowledge that Scripture characterizes it as strong, insidious, deceptive, both theologically and spiritually.

I will never count in order to satisfy myself, or to prove the correctness of the claim, that there are six hundred thirteen commandments in the Old Testament, and one thousand fifty in the New.[1] Those are interesting facts, and Bible students can delve deeply into the subject with great spiritual benefit. The "do's" and the "don't's" are always before us, in Scripture, literature, and sermon. They are to be prayerfully heeded by all. Here, however, I will move into a subject I call, "The Ten Greatest Temptations." I refer not to "breaking rules," but to mindsets, and "self-talk," which may well entice us into disastrous wrongdoing. These motivations may be conscious or unconscious. What I present has a manifest eschatological dimension, but also fully pertains to the living of each and every day. I will simply list these Temptations, and for clarity of expression will use the personal pronoun, "I." These Temptations are:

1. There is no personal, Creator God.
2. After my physical death I will not have to personally appear before a Creator God.
3. I will not literally have to give "an account" of my life.
4. I can truly and easily justify almost all of my sin and wrongdoing, including the "thoughts and imaginations of my heart" (Gen 6:5).

---

1. Eisenberg, *The 613 Mitzvot,* and Christian Assemblies, *1050 New Testament,* presented books on these matters.

5. My personal good deeds will be adequate to cancel or negate whatever wrong I have done.
6. There will be no literal, personal consequences for my sin or wrongdoing.
7. I will not be required to achieve anything like "perfect holiness."
8. I will not be required to achieve complete reconciliation with all other persons.
9. Since I "accepted Jesus Christ," God's forgiveness will automatically qualify me for an immediate beatified life.
10. I can, at the moment of my death, join the heavenly redeemed community "just as I am."

It goes without much theological comment to state that resisting temptation alone has never made anyone either holy or perfect. Christians must imitate Jesus Christ in resisting the call to sin, but must assertively move forward to create and promote righteousness. Historically, Christian renunciation has often produced a passivity, and a general reluctance to "face the world." But the world is sinful and broken, sad and alienated, demanding the best from believers' witness, actions, and prayers. Jesus often went away to pray and to renew his spiritual energy, but he returned and unstoppably embraced with robust vigor the pain and suffering all around him. A wonderful summary of his life was penned in a verse from the Book of Acts, and 10:38 gently affirms in great understatement: "God anointed Jesus of Nazareth with the Holy Spirit and with power, and he went about doing good."

In the Foundational Principles, I listed these as categories in which Jesus Christ demonstrated perfect holiness: faith, worship, service, trust, love, obedience. This accomplishment is exponentially more than simply "doing good." The list gives followers a roadmap for understanding and undertaking the mandated arduous, but blessing-filled journey to our own perfect holiness. Everything here is both inward- and outward-looking, deep contemplation lived out in energetic action.

On the Christian Calendar, Lent is always the forty days before Easter. It has been understood as a most serious time of spiritual preparation for the glorious Day of Resurrection. Its prominent themes have been self-examination, denial, and sacrifice. The season replicates the salient features of the life of Jesus Christ—service, sacrifice, and suffering, then followed by the wondrous power of Resurrection. A phrase used by devotees and heard throughout Christendom is, "giving up," that is, what is the believer willing to renounce or stop during Holy Lent, and that as an indication of devotion to the Lord. Many answers are given and vocally, from chocolate to alcohol to video games and television. I have a dear friend who will not shave during the forty days. More that once he has stated that, "After all Jesus did for us, I can do this for him." To be sure his devotional practice includes more than putting away his razor! Even so, that is a common enough example of the things Christians are thinking during this time of reflection.

I disparage nothing here, and am quite certain that there is joy in heaven over the smallest expression of sacrifice and self-effacement. I simply join the chorus of those who in recent years, especially in Protestantism, have added a few choice words to the liturgy of Lent. "What will I give up?" must be followed quickly by, "What will I add?" What to stop is highly commendable. What to start, even more so. That balanced reflection is more in line with Biblical teaching, and solidly imitative of the active, socially responsive life of the Nazarene. Resisting temptation is a command of God; so is the marching order to go into all the world. Through the Incarnate Union, Jesus Christ did both. Followers seeking holy perfection can do no less.

18

Soteriology at Chalcedon

For many of the ideas in this essay, I am indebted to the classic work by R. V. Sellers: *The Council of Chalcedon: A Historical and Doctrinal Survey.*[1]

The five hundred-plus bishops, monks, and other interested persons who arrived at Chalcedon in October, 451 CE, came armed with well-articulated views on both the Person and Work of Jesus Christ. When they left the seaside town in November, 451 CE, they had given the Church the monumental Creed of Chalcedon. Remarkably, however, the learned ecclesiastics wrote only of the Person; no word came forth on the Work. They penned nothing on the crucial theological issue of just how the Person actually "saves." That theology has not been put into universally accepted creedal language to this day.

Defining the Person correctly came first as a most urgent consideration. Historical necessity was forcing the issue, for many "heretical" views were vying for attention, and unless the ecumenical Council produced an Orthodox view, the chaos, confusion, and division would only worsen. The congregants were determined to stem that tide, and, in many ways, that was the salutary outcome.

But in the end, the heretics did not simply acquiesce and skulk away. They retreated into their separate enclaves and communities, continuing to exert a huge influence, and for centuries to

---

1. Sellers, *Council of Chalcedon,* 132–203.

come—even into our own. The Creed of Chalcedon was accepted by a majority, but not by all, of Christendom.

Soteriology was everywhere present at Chalcedon. It was discussed, debated, and argued. Nothing, however, was written down for the larger church, for in actuality, it could not be. The dominant three basic views found there were hopelessly irreconcilable. To be sure, other ideas and opinions were, have been, and are put forth. Reviewing them all is not my purpose, but I will comment briefly on the basic and most widely held theologies at Chalcedon. Personally, I have always relied heavily on the Creed for my understanding of Incarnation, and I find it extremely compelling to reflect upon the fact that several "Soteriologies" were lying just below the surface of its magnificent wording.

It has proven useful to identify these theologies with cities, though naturally proponents of each school were scattered throughout the vast Mediterranean area. The metropolitan centers were Rome, Alexandria, and Antioch. Other cities and monasteries sent delegates, of course, and in time all the attending ecclesiastics dutifully arrived and the heady work began apace.

The Doctrine of Soteriology may be usefully, if simply, explored by asking two questions: One, what is the plight of humanity? Two, how does Jesus Christ remedy or resolve this plight? I will use this format in my cursory remarks.

The city of Alexandria was long famous as a center for vaunted, intellectual discussions. Not surprisingly, the believers there took a philosophical approach to things Christian. They determined that the main problem for persons was finitude and mortality, and that the entirety of human nature required a very specific redemptive action. The Soteriological focus was on people in the aggregate, and Jesus Christ graciously came to redeem the race collectively from its bane and blight. His Work was essentially the deification of composite human nature, in a transcendent, metaphysical way. A summary phrase resonated with the Alexandrians, and explains their interest: "God became human, so that humanity could become God."

While this approach stirs the intellect, and while humanity is surely condemned to impermanence and death, there is no Biblical justification or support for this diagnostic gibberish. It is difficult to determine how these North African minds could align the Person presented in the Gospels and the Creed with such an odd, vague, curious task and Work. There is no Scriptural evidence for Jesus Christ speaking or acting in a way commensurate with his desire to accomplish such an outcome.

The Romans present at Chalcedon brought the Soteriology which has been dominant in all Western Theology, and also in its sixteenth-century stepchild, the Protestant Reformation. The human plight is the near-criminal status of all sinners. They have violated God's law, and the just punishment is the condemnation of eternal separation. The remedy for this woeful situation is thus described as a legal transaction wherein someone appeases God's wrath, vicariously accepts the sinners' fate, and sets the individual sinner free. The One to do that meritorious work was, of course, Jesus Christ. God declared his death on the Cross an acceptable sacrifice, atonement, and penalty payment on behalf of all who, with a pure heart, would accept the proffered salvation.

The Western view of Soteriology has been pieced together by Scripture proof-texting, omitting whatever is at odds with its ironclad thinking. But its presuppositions are flawed beyond repair. It is impossible to imagine this "Plan of Salvation" emerging from the counsels of Holy Trinity before the Creation of the world and persons. If God's wrath must be appeased, and if the Second Person of the Incarnation is truly the same God, a logical analysis becomes a dizzying exercise in contradictions. How does God appease the Incarnate God in any action of the Incarnation? Serious thinkers may try to imaginatively reconstruct the Trinity's pre-Creation deliberations relative to this scheme of redemption, but the result can only be cognitively confusing with no satisfactory intellectual or theological conclusions.

Roman ideas do not jibe with the Person described in the Creed for the simple reason that nothing in its wording interfaces with this accounting-transaction Theology. The Creedal concept of the Person does not match that definition of his Work. The ideas are irreconcilable.

The Antiochenes viewed the plight in moral-ethical terms, advancing the notion that persons are in bondage to sin through the misuse of their God-given free wills. Every human is of Adam's race, and thus a fallen sinner. Salvation could come only when a new, Second Adam appeared, one who would keep God's law perfectly, without sin. Persons found "in" Christ, the Second Adam, through baptism, and obedient membership in the church, would be seen by God as redeemed and saved eternally by this new Incarnate One. Nothing in Creedal language seemed a mismatch for this Antiochene thinking.

These three ancient Conciliar ideologies and their proponents were pleased with their new Creed, and would have heartily approved the later additions made at Constantinople decades later. But to review: the Alexandrians saw Soteriology as a philosophical-metaphysical event. The Romans affirmed salvation through a "legal" transaction. Antiochenes taught that salvation was an achievement, as it had been for Jesus through the Second Person. Soon enough the gifted but testy ecclesiastics, from all over the known world, left Chalcedon professing one, ecumenical faith in the newly-defined Jesus Christ. It was a remarkable achievement, directed, no doubt, by the very Holy Spirit of God.

19

The Birth of Jesus Christ 1

ANY DISCUSSION OF THE Person of Jesus Christ eventually must include questions about his birth. They will be considered here and in the next essay.

According to the Gospel of Luke, 4:22, the bystanders in Nazareth, after hearing Jesus preach asked in astonishment, "Is this not Joseph's son?" Matthew gives the wording, "Is this not the carpenter's son?" (13:55). Mark's Gospel says something quite different: "Is this not the carpenter, the son of Mary?" (6:3). Mark fails to mention Joseph for reasons about which we can only speculate, and focuses on Mary. As latter day saints, we can also ask with the audience, "Was Jesus the son of Joseph?" How?

The New Testament did not give a crystal clear definition of the Person of Jesus Christ, but the nascent church worked on the matter diligently. At Chalcedon, it put words of faith in an orderly fashion, shedding much illumination on the many aspects of what had become a major, and problematic issue. Their declaration here is striking: the Incarnate One was fully human and fully divine, born of Mary, the Virgin God-bearer. Believers have professed this Creed since it was written in 431 CE. My concern here is to look closely at the relationship between the concept of Virgin Birth and the affirmation that Jesus Christ was "fully human."

Scientists of human reproduction report that at conception the genetic makeup of a person is complete. The male sperm cell brings half of the required chromosomes to the female egg, which contains the other half. The combined forty-six chromosomes provide all the essential genetic information to the diploid offspring. The gestation period has begun.

While the Fathers at Chalcedon had no knowledge of these facts, they would have found them highly interesting, but also superfluous, even irrelevant. It cannot be doubted that these worthies ardently believed the stories in Matthew and Luke which confirmed a miraculous conception and a Virginal birth. Accordingly, they would have declared that the facts of science do no more than give glory to God. Furthermore, in that holy conception, God's Spirit could provide and effect whatever was necessary for a so-called scientific pregnancy to occur. Believers in Virgin Birth have espoused similar views for all of Christian history. Of course, those who do not believe in the miraculous birth can also affirm the same things about the ability and power of God.

Believers in Virgin Birth are not much concerned over Jesus Christ's relationship to Joseph. They look askance at the question, "Is this Joseph's son?" They honor the older carpenter variously as Patron Saint of the Unborn, Patron Saint of Families, a quiet, hard working servant, always in the background. At the Manger Scene he is mute, formidable, stalwart. In our era we speak of a male figure who adopts, or takes in a ward, as a guardian or step-parent. Though there is no exact term for him in this unique relationship, Joseph has generally been so designated, and for all centuries. Regardless of his title, he does his protective, silent duty until, mysteriously, he disappears from the Gospel records, with no word on his demise, or on the location of a burial site, which would have instantly been sacred ground. Christians remain grateful to Saint Joseph, even as it is acknowledged that he is largely unknowable and inscrutable, forever in the wings of the Incarnational stage.

But the question of the hometown neighbors should not be summarily dismissed. It should, rather, be put in bold relief. To be sure, these Nazarenes were only momentarily dazzled, then so annoyed and enraged that they sent the "carpenter" packing, under a hail of threat, scorn, and murderous denunciation. They hastily reconstructed their initial interpretation of the man, and quickly forgot their quizzical wonderment about his origins. Their question remains with us, however.

For all believers in miraculous conception and birth, every answer given demands an asterisk or a footnote. It would maintain that the Incarnate One does not have a "human" father, nor is one required. The assertion would announce that Jesus Christ has no earthly father, but most definitely an earthly mother. But is this claim an essential tenet of the Theology of the Incarnation? Can one born of a Virgin truly be existentially relevant to the lives of ordinary, "normally born" persons? Do properties imparted and inherent in such a miraculous conception and birth preclude and contradict the words of Scripture and Creed, that he was "like us in all respects apart from sin"? Indeed, was Jesus' sinless life at all possible without facilitation by characteristics provided and empowered by divine participation?

After this dizzying plethora of questions, it is incumbent to recall that the Second Person of the Trinity is not "born"; the birth is of Jesus of Nazareth. And further, that the Incarnation is a Union concurring into one Personal Presence and one Personal Identity. It is, therefore, not logical necessity for Christian Faith to affirm and declare that only through Virgin Birth can the Son of God be Incarnately joined to the "Son of Man." Incarnation is ultimately a mystery, a miracle, and beyond human knowing. We cannot assume to know the process for its introduction into this "world below." Nor should we claim such knowledge.

The hometown Nazarenes drove Jesus away, quickly forgetting their wonderment about this amazing talent and his ordinary upbringing by ordinary parents. We, however, must not forget the question, but ask it in a much more inviting, generous way. Regardless of the unusual facts surrounding his natal day, we are here dealing with the Incarnate Lord Jesus Christ.

20

The Birth of Jesus Christ 2

EVEN IF THOUGHTFUL CHRISTIANS acknowledge that God cannot be "born," the theological horizon always opens to reveal the necessity of more deeply investigating human birth, including the possibility of a Virgin Birth. In my Propositions I affirm that God is the sole originator of the Incarnation, and that Jesus of Nazareth contributes nothing to effect the Union. This statement now demands more elaboration.

However, some Christians believe that Mary of Nazareth does contribute to the Union, and should be honored for her acquiescence to being impregnated and bearing the Son of God. Chalcedon identifies her in near celestial terms: "Mary, the Virgin God-bearer." From this kind of thinking she may be referred to as "Coredemptress," and "Mediatrix." In her humility she literally brings the Savior into the world, carrying and nurturing him in her perfectly pure womb.

Marian Theology and devotion, itself fascinating, tender, and often beautiful, is not pertinent to this discussion, other than to note that it clearly teaches a significant contribution to the Incarnation by the very human mother of Jesus. At Chalcedon the Fathers added, probably for pressing political reasons, the highly-charged Greek theological term, *Theotokos*. This language can only be understood as declaring that humanity was inextricably intermixed in the initial Incarnation event. In fact, some translations of the Creed of Chalcedon use the objectionable and misguided words, "Mary, the Mother of God." Jesus of Nazareth has a mother; God does not.

Protestants who confidently believe in miraculous conception and birth still see no merit in referring to Mary in any such honorific language, other than gratefully acknowledging her exceptional part in bearing Jesus Christ and contributing to his maturational care and development. They assert that Mary was indeed "full of grace," not because of her angelic, moral probity, but because she was visited by God. That alone makes one blessed. Aside from consideration of Mary's physical mothering, what must be considered vis-à-vis the Incarnation? We turn our singular attention to the idea and concept of Virgin Birth, where four issues arise.

1. Must one affirm the necessity for Virgin Birth in the Incarnation?
2. Must one believe in the Virgin Birth in order to be a Christian?
3. What is the Biblical record on this divine conception and birth?
4. Is there evidence that Jesus believed he was so conceived?
These points follow in response.

1. It is not necessary to affirm belief in the Virgin Birth in the Incarnation. This point has been made repeatedly here.
2. It is not necessary to believe in the Virgin Birth in order to be a Christian. Untold numbers believe in the Incarnation without belief in that event.
3. Incarnation began in the human zygote, regardless of how that zygote was produced. The coming together of God and man, by whatever process, was entirely the work of God.
4. A miraculous conception by Mary is not mentioned in either the Gospel of John or the Gospel of Mark. It is vacuous to assert that the audiences of these Gospels were already familiar with the fact. By way of the same logic, they should also have been quite familiar with much of the material subsequently presented by both John and Mark. Why were they written if everyone already knew those facts?
5. To the Johannine editors, composers of the highly philosophical, esoteric Prologue, such a datum would have been an irresistible and highly prized addition to the story of the divine

Logos appearing on earth. Why would they have omitted such a stunning fact?

6. Christian Faith can understand and affirm that in deeply devout piety, Matthew and Luke created and produced Birth and Infancy Narratives, and that for any number of reasons. Their constructs are so dissimilar that there must have been two independent sources for their stories, which are forever lost to us. If their redactors were the authors, they are themselves the sources.

7. If it is affirmed that the audiences of John or Mark, the first Gospel, later learned of the miraculous birth, the claim is irrelevant because historically without any factual evidence.

8. The Virgin Birth is never mentioned again in the entirety of twenty-five books of the New Testament. This is impossible to account for if the story had any claim to authenticity. As an actual fact, it could absolutely not be relegated to minor or insignificant status by the writers or editors of Scripture texts. Virgin Birth would have been considered an earth-shaking mighty act of God, and would provide an immovable foundation for the claims of Christian Theology.

9. The Apostle Paul wrote a large number of New Testament books. He uses expected, ordinary language referencing the birth of Jesus Christ: "God sent forth his son, born of a woman" (Gal 4:4–5). Had he the more spectacular, miraculous birth data, he would have interjected it precisely at this point. It would be cherished data for his basic and entire theology, and unthinkable that he would not mention it, time and again. He would simply have felt compelled to comment upon it at considerable length. He did not. He wrote many things, proudly and powerfully, but on this he spoke not a word.

10. The most important fact regarding Scripture reference to the Virgin Birth is this: In the four Gospels Jesus Christ makes no mention of this dogma or belief. In none of the familial conversations with Mary and his siblings, nor in any intimate discussion with disciples, is the matter mentioned. Given the Johannine preoccupation with a Messiah in constant contact with God, from whom he receives personal supernatural

instruction and guidance, it would appear certain that those editors and redactors would have included such a paramount affidavit for divine legitimacy. The Jesus Christ of that Gospel would have vigorously and repeatedly shared such astonishing information, as his custom was to provocatively report such heavenly news.

11. Christian Theologies of the Virgin Birth have never demonstrated the crucial significance or importance of such a doctrine. Its implications remain vague and inarticulate, even to those who have written about it exhaustively. It appears as an ancillary doctrine in their theology, never convincingly attached to the main features.

12. The most conservative Christian Theology cannot demonstrate that there can be no Incarnation without a Virgin Birth. The relationship between the two cannot be shown to be necessary or obvious, only that it is "taught in the Bible."

13. The necessity to believe such a doctrine is incumbent only upon those who believe that the Birth and Infancy Narratives are the starting point for all Incarnational Theology, and that they are literally true and factual in their reporting.

14. The term "Virgin" in Virgin Mary may unhesitatingly be spoken in Creed and Confession, with the understanding that it is a spiritual title rather than a reference to Mary's physical and moral condition before the holy conception.

15. Christianity must never make decisions about believers' faith commitment and discipleship dependent upon belief in this doctrine.

16. Christian disciples may believe the doctrine, reject its literalness, or remain agnostic about it, while still proclaiming that "Jesus Christ is Lord and Savior."

17. The Blessed Holy Trinity can initiate Incarnation in many ways, from male-female union to Virgin Birth.

18. The entire New Testament implies that the details of his birth had little significance or importance to the life and ministry of Jesus Christ. It is therefore, irrelevant to fundamental Christian Theology.

21

Resurrection "Proofs"

AT ONE OF MY alma maters, a Bible Instructor claimed that the folded napkin in the empty tomb was a proof that Jesus Christ had risen (John 20:7). I have hoped that he really knew better, and would not propose that doctrine in Scripture can be proved by reference to that very Scripture itself. This approach is not permissible, is anti-intellectual, and actually hurts so-called "Christian Apologetics." One can account for a folded face cloth in many ways other than putting it forth as evidence for a cataclysmic, earth-changing event!

Everyone offering "proofs" for the Resurrection is merely presenting supporting data for what one already believes. Determined efforts to assist someone to "believe it" are to be commended, but there are, of course, no proofs in the sense that the word is defined in logic and the hard sciences. If indeed those proofs actually proved anything, they would be convincing, irresistible, and irrefutable. Many more persons would profess faith in a Risen Lord. This would be the case unless those confronted were incorrigible and stubbornly refused to face inarguable reality. Nothing can be done in such cases. If it is countered that everyone with "a good heart" should believe, that notion is patently untrue, not to mention condescending in the extreme.

What is true is that God alone grants belief in the Resurrection of Jesus of Nazareth. This is a mysterious, divine working, which may surprisingly occur in unlikely circumstances, even when someone is offering up their vaunted proofs. Most self aware Christians will confess that they "found themselves believing," and that without much detailed analysis of either Scripture or Christian Theology. It is a holy, wholly unknowable affair!

Turning to those Scriptures, the point is instantly apparent that the basic, fundamental teaching on the Resurrection has nothing to do with proofs. Its message is simply that many persons, hundreds at least, believed it, and came to such faith in a remarkably short period of time. A dead man was alive again, they announced, and through their witness and the Election of Grace, God was stoking the spreading flame of Christianity.

Of course, retorts and objections can be made to the Scriptural reportage. For example, the body of Jesus of Nazareth could certainly have been stolen, leaving an empty tomb, and opening the disciples' grieving minds to all kinds of imaginings. It was clearly in the political interest of Rome and the Jews to do away with the corpse.

Then, too, mass hallucinations are known to have occurred many times in history, and large groups of emotional people can "see" and "believe" things to be true that are not. New Testament saints were not completely immune from falling prey to such mass hysteria. People have the psychological ability to "wish" things into existence.

Also, each Gospel reports the same basic fact, with significant differences in detail: the women were the first to appear at the empty tomb. They could have gone to the wrong tomb! Stranger things have happened. In 1 Corinthians 15, the Apostle Paul is handing on to others what was handed on to him. He shares a lengthy list of witnesses to the Resurrection. Curiously and inexplicably he makes no mention of these women. Perhaps the fact had not been related to him and naturally he could not include it. Or, perhaps he realized, and even believed, that women witnesses had no or little standing in certain circles. Their testimony would not "count," regardless. Whatever the reasons for Paul's omission, it is noteworthy in many ways.

There are, doubtless, several other objections and exceptions which could allow non-believers to resist any story, Biblical or otherwise, which announced the rejuvenation of one once convincingly dead. And yet, since proofs count for nothing to the incredulous, so, in contrary ways, these reasons do nothing to dissuade those who already affirm, "He is Risen!"

In concluding this I reassert that belief in Resurrection is a gift, wholly from God. So-called proofs do not account for, nor create, it. And no evidence against Resurrection is persuasive to a true believer. The New Testament teaches that multitudes believed the literalness of the event. The Holy Writ does not, however, attempt to prove it by any means which would be understood in the modern usage of the term. So, belief is a miraculous event, a result of what some theologians have called, Irresistible Grace. This simply means that since belief is a divine infusion, the believer cannot NOT believe! Then, such disciples should disdain proving the Easter message, and spend more time witnessing to it.

22

Incarnation's Dark Hours

THE THREE SYNOPTIC GOSPELS declare that while Jesus Christ was hanging on the Cross, the earth was overcome with darkness for three long hours (Matt 27:45; Mark 15:33; Luke 23:44–45). The cause of this meteorological phenomenon was assumed to be God. The symbolism is apparent enough: the earth and all its inhabitants should recognize the cosmic significance of the dark event now transpiring on Calvary. That spiritual message seems to have been lost on many of the onlookers, however, as they continued to jeer and slander the dying wretch. This is another example of God providing a revelation but not transparently revealing what it might "mean."

But perhaps the best symbolism for reflecting on the Theology of the Incarnation would have been something else: a display of complete darkness at 3 PM, the moment Jesus of Nazareth breathed his last. Certainly, an interpretive pall descended on every human being at that fateful hour.

A term from modern military and intelligence jargon has become part of common parlance: "going dark." Its short definition is that all communication has ceased between entities, organizations, or human assets with whom previous dialogue had been held. One party suddenly disappears and all channels for further contact are thereby closed. For Christian Faith, something like this happened from 3 PM Friday to the Sunday morning of Resurrection. I call this, "Incarnation's Dark Hours."

Theologians of the Christian Church have had a relatively safe and easy time getting the Nazarene through his thirty-odd years to that Friday afternoon on the "Old Rugged Cross." However, these thinkers have not done well dealing with the events immediately following: death, burial, resurrection, resurrection appearances, and the Second Person returned to heaven, reincorporated into the Holy Trinity. My belief that theology is interpretive speculation is highly applicable here. As long as speculation is carefully articulated and devotionally grounded, believers have permission to plumb the depths of the greatest mysteries, like this one. Their findings, suggestions, and results must be noted as tentative, of course.

We are forced to speculate here for several obvious reasons. Everything about that Friday afternoon begins with the fact that God cannot die. From that certainty, all questions begin and all problems arise. Second, no writer or editor of New Testament texts offers any data on this subject. There was no revelation here, and those writers obviously chose not to comment on the matter, except in a few obscure texts from two verses in the Epistle of Peter. New Testament materials go quickly from death on the Cross to Resurrection morn, and understandably so. Following suit, judicious and wise theologians have left this topic in the hazy area of unknowable.

All believers acknowledge that assuredly we cannot discover what happened in those dreary, crushing hours before Sunday sunrise. Yet, we humbly recall a remark attributed to the great Saint Augustine of Hippo. When considering the Doctrine of the Trinity, he quipped that to keep from saying nothing he would say something![1] This is a kind of tacit permission for us lesser minds to think, speak, even write.

Since God as Second Person of the Trinity cannot die, these are some questions which then arise. They all begin with the same wording: What is the relationship between that Second Person and. . .

1. What happened on the Cross at 3 PM?
2. The body taken from the Cross and entombed?
3. The body resurrected on Easter Morn?

1. Augustine, *"Augustine of Hippo Quotes,"* 1.

4. The One now resurrected, thereafter encountered by witnesses and disciples?
5. The One who ascended into heaven?
6. The One now seated at "The Right Hand of the Father"?
7. The One who is simultaneously "always with" his disciples?

In appropriately perplexed ignorance, I make these observations. God the Second Person did not die, but Jesus of Nazareth did. The body was recognized after its death, and then solemnly entombed by shocked and stricken disciples. The resurrected body was also recognized and readily identified as that of Jesus of Nazareth. Events transpiring thereafter were interpreted by disciples as evidence that the now Resurrected One possessed similar powers, abilities, and insights as the One who had been crucified, dead, and buried.

There is, of course, no theological information that the eternally living Second Person "lay" in a borrowed tomb for three days with a deceased body. That is an exceedingly odd, even macabre thought. Then did the Son indeed leave the body there, and return to enliven it Sunday morning? In any event, it is again noted that Jesus of Nazareth could have had no part whatsoever in his own resurrection. That happening was the mighty power of God ALONE.

We have no information about what happened to the "body" of Jesus of Nazareth. In the resurrection appearances the body known and recognized by disciples is essentially a duplicate of the pre-crucifixion embodiment. As we have seen, the New Testament records make this point explicitly.

In this regard, Holy Trinity had the power to transform this, or any body, into a glorious new one. That fact is not in dispute, and is a foundational understanding for belief in any personal and universal resurrection. The Apostle Paul writes of his own non-revealed, speculative ideas about these "bodies" in 1 Corinthians 15. His "guesses" are as good as any!

A comment on 1 Peter is pertinent here. In 3:18–19, the writer pens some of the strangest passages in the New Testament: ". . .Christ . . . being put to death in the flesh, was made alive by the Spirit, by which he also went and preached to the spirits in prison

. . . ." Is this passage relevant to our wonderments about the relationship between the Second Person and the body of Jesus of Nazareth? Some have thought so.

From the earliest days of Christianity, many have pondered what the Son of God may have done between the death on the Cross and the Resurrection event. Using passages like this, and a few other allusive texts, an imaginative, creative story was spawned. It saw Jesus Christ venturing into the nether world of Purgatory, not Hell, to inform the soon to be heaven bound saints that the reason for their ultimate glorification was standing before them. The Savior who died on the Cross had come to set them free and to lead them joyously to their celestial home. Apparently, the travelling Lord then returned to earth to appear dramatically on the Day of Resurrection. The form of this new identity or new being was not described in the details.

This truly fascinating bit of apocryphal Christian history is a perfect example of what can occur when fertile minds respond to genuine puzzlements. They may even create dogma to then be embraced by the faithful. In any event, it is a delightful part of church lore, with the unofficial title, "The Harrowing of Hell." Christ left the Cross, led souls from Purgatory to heaven, then returned to resuscitate the dead Jesus of Nazareth.

First Peter 3:18–19 is hopelessly difficult to exegete, but minimally suggests a vital, genuine separation between the Second Person and the deceased Jesus. If God the Son went, "in the Spirit" to a place for the dead, we can safely say he was not "in the flesh" of the entombed human Jesus. We can also assume that any "spirit in prison" in that Hadean realm, was equally not a person of flesh and blood. The verses are not important for presenting an itinerary of goings and comings, but because they suggest a severing of the Incarnational relationship at the Friday afternoon death of Jesus. That makes logical theological sense even as the very idea is fraught with imponderable questions and accompanying implications.

One more thought on this opaque issue. If the Incarnation terminated at Jesus' death, and the Second Person was then again out and about in the earth and the cosmos, it could be stated that God resurrected Jesus of Nazareth as an entirely new, unique being, now independent of the Trinity. That is a proposal which few could accept, and needs no further exploration here.

All Christians recognize empathically that the long minutes from Friday to Sunday were bleak and desperate for the grieving community of believers. If they were in utter darkness, they would soon discover that Holy Trinity was not. On Easter Morning, the darkness fled and shadows withdrew, as disciples shouted, "He is Risen!" What happened in those long, painful hours of waiting is the stuff of cautious theological enthrallment.

23

Living Incarnationally

I.

From my reading I have concluded that Ludwig Wittgenstein had no formal theological training. However, for the greatest philosopher of the twentieth century, school records and transcripts would be quite irrelevant. His was a mind which could have mastered, in short order, what would take other learned thinkers years to acquire. He was, quite simply, a genius. With all due respect to Wittgenstein, knowing theology is not necessarily knowing God, nor does it imply a pious life.

Though a non-believer, he did think about theology. Fortunately he left a few jottings and sentences in his one published volume, and also in boxes of unpublished papers. In his *Tractatus Logico-Philosophicus*, which was printed during his lifetime, he demonstrated that philosophy was not just a collection of concepts or propositions; it was a way, a method, an activity for making sense of those things.[1]

In another work, published after his death as *The Philosophical Investigations*, he wrote three words which he curiously put in parentheses: (Theology as grammar).[2] In that work he quickly

1. Wittgenstein, *Tractatus*, 109.
2. Wittgenstein, *Investigations*, 373.

went on to other matters and concerns, leaving the cryptic remark dangling in a tantalizing way for all who stumble across it. I believe we should not rush beyond it, but perhaps "camp out," and think deeply about where the comment might take us. I want to do that here, but I will combine the phrases, changing the words slightly for my purposes: "Theology is an activity, a specific way of making sense of things. Theology is also a grammar for living life." I think Wittgenstein, the Austrian thinker, would not strongly object to what I am doing here, and would likely offer penetrating input where he thought I could analyze better and say things more clearly. Whatever else he was, he was a consummate logician.

He knew as well that the discipline of philosophy had produced libraries stocked with books and tomes chocked full of those aforementioned propositions, concepts, affirmations, and syllogisms. Likewise a glance at a few shelves of theological texts would have given him the very same confirming insight. The latter are full of analyses, interpretations, creeds, dogma, sermons, and propositions. Whatever does he mean by declaring that philosophy (and theology) is not merely this body of material, but is, rather, a way of doing something with it? Clearly he is making a distinction between these massive bodies of intellectual production and what the material can be "used for" in one's life. This is a profound distinction, and is fraught with implications for all things in theology, particularly the Theology of the Incarnation. The Doctrine must actually inform life existentially.

II.

Wittgenstein's distinction can be applied to Christian Faith by use of a simple example. Each week millions of believers recite one of several Creeds. The most often heard is likely, "The Apostles Creed." In saying the words we have many options. We can read them and make an instant pronouncement that it is theology, plain and simple. That is decidedly correct. But we can go beyond that observation and wonder, "Does this ancient aggregation of words have anything whatsoever to do with the way I am living my daily

life?" And with that we are on the trail of basic, fundamental understanding and human wisdom.

At a personal level, as an ordained minister, I can, not surprisingly, recite the words by heart. But I have many options here. I
can say the Creed without meaning it. I can confess that I do not
believe any of it. I can join the confessing congregation, all the while
thinking of my coming luncheon, or trip to the lake. Truly, I can be
both absent-minded and disingenuous. I can take the historically
important theology and make it into any number of things other
than its intended purpose and usage.

On the other hand, I can repeat words such as, "I believe
in God the Father Almighty, and in his only Son, our Lord Jesus
Christ," in total self awareness, indicating that this ancient language
expresses something eternally true, and that ought to provide an
undergirding for the actions which should follow upon such an ut-
terly profound recitation and confession. I can be gripped by the
words in a truly existential, experiential way, and thereafter better
organize my entire life, because I have once again professed them
before God and in public with other believers.

Theology is the body of data. Theology is also the way we live
vis-à-vis the data. They cannot be separated, even as we can both
see and describe the difference Wittgenstein was brilliantly noting.
Even if our examples differ wildly!

III

Edgar Guest, the prolific poet wrote, seriously or not, I cannot
say, but the quote is immortal: "I would rather see a sermon than
hear one."[3] I always chuckle at that, thinking the worst: the person
just does not want to attend a religious service where a sermon
might actuality be preached! But I can also be more charitable and
declare that the quip contains spiritual insight. The speaker is making the point that how one lives one's life is the important thing.
The sermon should be translated into observable, public actions as

---

3. Guest, *Collected Poems*, 599.

one attempts to live out the message preached. If that is homespun wisdom, it is solid gold.

There is a caveat, however. Living a sermon or a Creed does presuppose the theology. In other words, the preached theology or the spoken Creed become the data-filled media which inform the lifestyle. Had Wittgenstein heard the humorous and quaint remark cited above, he may well have said that that was exactly what he was talking about. Theology is data, but that same theology is also the very grammar of life. It informs and tells us how to live intentionally. (Then with honest self-analysis we should ask if others can determine our theology by how we live day by day. Can they discern that we believe God was in Jesus of Nazareth? It is a shockingly significant wonderment.)

Perhaps we can now see better the great wisdom in labelling theology, "grammar." That term is from the study of linguistics, and not unfamiliar to the youngest pupil studying a language. Its applicability to theology and lifestyle is quite transparent. But this is a vital additional point: when humans communicate verbally, they rarely focus self-consciously on the grammar. The rules are well enough known that the grammar is only a tacit ingredient in the conversation or written communication. Similarly, those who believe in the Incarnation do not ordinarily go around "talking theology" in normal human exchange. The inward undergirding, foundational belief is always there, however, informing the thoughts, words, and actions. Despite the sad fact that Christians are sinners, not always faithful to things believed or professed, their calling is clear. And certainly the wider world needs desperately to see Incarnational Theology lived out.

Many New Testament texts declare this kind of basic truth. Jesus Christ said, "You should be known by your fruit" (Mt 7). This is not about horticultural skills, but about what can be seen in one's outward life. And Paul penned a beautiful, profound passage in 2 Corinthians 3:2: "You are our living epistles." This is not about precision in penmanship or stenography. It is about boldly allowing one's life to be "read" as a consistent set of actions before peers and strangers. Wittgenstein's words well reflect many themes contained in Holy Writ, likely unbeknownst to him.

IV

There is no greater awareness in life than that the Blessed Holy Trinity lovingly became Incarnate in a human being. There is no greater confession than that one believes it to be the case, and with all one's heart. When it is realized that one has been chosen by God to both believe and to confess, the claim on that life becomes powerful and grace-filled. Everything is different for time and eternity. And everyone believing and confessing can understand immediately what I mean by an essay titled, "Living Incarnationally."

24

Closing Thoughts

In the end, all theology, including mine, is speculative. There is no "scientific method" to validate any truth claim for verifiability, other than the believer's internal witness of the Holy Spirit, and the corporate equivalent witness in a community of faith. Even then history must be remembered, for there has never been uniformity of thought about particular doctrines, much less agreement on the work of the Spirit. Christianity seems condemned to division, despite the pleas of Scripture, even of the Lord himself. "Being one in faith" is as elusive as ever. And yet, the modern Church has displayed a general comfort with, and tolerance for, differing individual expressions of theological opinion and interpretation.

In two previous books I attempted to demonstrate what I am affirming again, and what is too often lost sight of: every legitimate doctrine of Christian Theology must find its locus and foundation in understandings of and about the Blessed Holy Trinity. No doctrine stands alone, outside those considerations. In *The Love of God and the Age to Come: No Eternal Hell*, I declared that all views of any life in any age to come can be articulated only with reference to views held about God.[1] In *God and the Twelve Problems of Evil: Into Great Mystery*, I stated that all efforts to deal with the intractable Problem of Evil must begin and end with God.[2] Likewise, the

1. Vaughan, *Love of God*, 35–37.
2. Vaughan, *Twelve Problems*, 21–23.

Closing Thoughts

Doctrines of both Soteriology and Christology can have clarity only as they interface with a consistent, properly Biblical view of God.

That is, of course, the rub. Views of God differ dramatically. Since that is the case, theologies of the Incarnation do as well. It is easily observable that understandings of God at variance with mine will produce other interpretive positions. As a believer and writer, I am quite comfortable with that, trusting that my views will be given fair consideration in the great dialogical arena of both the church and World Religions. I have stated that Incarnation is an action of a loving God on behalf of "the whole world," not just for Christianity and its many branches.

Much of Christian Theology reaches a very misguided conclusion, though it is often completely unexpressed: It does not matter how we understand the Person of Jesus Christ as long as his Work is effective and efficacious. Why should we obsess in attempting to define that Person as long as his death on the Cross is salvific? I have been at pains to show that such notions inadequately grasp the cosmic depth of Christianity. Any theology that focuses exclusively on his death dismissively disparages his Life. That entire life is the Work of Jesus Christ. His holy perfection redeems by being eternalized by God. We must "walk in his steps" until our salvation is complete. I have referenced the glorious fact that Scripture assures believers that we are helped in this difficult task by an internal spiritual power, "Christ in you, the hope of glory" (Col 1:27). The case can further be made that we need the positive effect of likeminded believers in a fellowship of worship, learning, and service. Personal change always comes through acts of ministry and mercy. Someone rightly said that in visiting the sick, we likely do very little for them, but much for our own souls. It seems so.

Perhaps we should think of the Incarnation as a miracle. We cannot explain how it occurred, only comment on the results. All interpretations and suggestions address only the tangent, the periphery, the edges of the Doctrine. No one can fathom or experience the center, the divine core, the eternal mystery. We may be like the blind man who was asked who healed him. He said, "I do not know, but I know I can see!" (John 9:25). We may know a little more—but not much. For one, I am content.

25

Finally. . . .

OVER SOME YEARS NOW, my Incarnational Muddle has become less so, and my views on the Person and Work of Jesus Christ have become more mature and more central to my life and work. The great Puritan preacher, John Robinson, (1576–1625), claimed there was much more light to break forth from the Word of God.[1] I do not doubt it, and much of it will inevitably relate to understanding the Incarnation. If disciple means "learner," I must forever be one.

The greatest work of Christian allegory is *The Pilgrim's Progress* by John Bunyan.[2] I have been touched by many of its scenes. Near the end of the very long book, we read of travelers Christian and Hopeful, journeying on from this World to the Next. They can see ahead of them the desired, beautiful Celestial City. But between the Pilgrims and its shining Gates is a perilous, most fearful River. There are no bridges by which to cross. The water appears deep, and at its sight the sojourners were "much astounded," gripped by fear. Guides reminded them that they could not come to the City Gates unless they passed through that forbidding River. So, Hopeful and Christian cautiously but dutifully step into the raging water. Fierce waves splash and roar. Hopeful has entered first and his companion courageously follows. Then suddenly Christian's worst fears are realized: he begins to sink. He cries out to friend Hopeful in urgent

1. Robinson, *Pilgrim Spirit,* no pagination.
2. Bunyan, *Pilgrim's Progress,* Section 10.

despair, "All the billows and waves go over me!" But brave Hopeful acknowledges the plaintive cry, and shouts back to his struggling friend most remarkable words of comfort and courage. The saving words are these: "Be of good cheer, my Brother. I can touch the bottom, and it is good and sound."

I am persuaded that after all is said and all is written, by professional theologians or fledglings like me, true believers can indeed rest, for this world and the next, upon something sound and rock solid. When he wrote these words in 1 Corinthians 3:11, the great Apostle Paul was not approaching a river and there thinking theologically. He was, rather, reflecting upon the greatest adventure and journey of all: living a life pleasing to the Triune God. He claimed that in order to accomplish this arduous but glorious feat, one had to realize and accept a single, eternal fact: "For no one can lay a foundation other than that which is already laid, Jesus Christ." Millions of persons have gratefully heard the Apostle, and have agreed that at least on this most vital matter, he is unquestionably and profoundly correct. The journey is long and hard, and sometimes the River is treacherous and fearful, but they have agreed with all Pilgrims, and with dear Hopeful—the foundation is indeed good and sound and solid.

Bibliography

Augustine of Hippo. *"Augustine of Hippo Quotes."* Quoteslyfe.com, 2021. <htps:www.quoteslyfe.com/quote/Yet-we-must-say-something-when-there-9913>.

Beaumont, Douglas. *The Origin of "In Essentials Unity."* Theology, Philosophy, Apologetics. douglasbeaumont.com, 2013.

Bunyan, John. *The Pilgrim's Progress.* Ross-shire, Scotland: The Covenant of Grace, 2014. covenantofgrace.com.

Carroll, Lewis. *Alice's Adventures in Wonderland.* London: Macmillan, 1865.

The Creed of Chalcedon. Translated by Charles K. Robinson. Uncopyrighted. Durham NC, no date.

Eisenberg, Ronald L. *The 613 Mitzvot: A Contemporary Guide to the Commandments of Judaism.* Rockville: Schreiber, 2005.

Feiner, Johannes. *A Common Catechism: A Book of Christian Faith.* New York: Seabury, 1975.

Guest, Edgar A. *Collected Verse.* New York: Buccaneer Press, 1976.

Later Creeds: The Creed of Constantinople. Christia File Archives, 3. Uncopyrighted, 1994. listserv@asum.inre.asu.edu.

Luther, Martin. *The Babylonian Captivity of the Church.* Translated by Albert T.W. Scheinhaeuser. Chicago: 2011. http://self.gutenberg.org/.

Melancthon, Philip. *Commonplaces: Loci communes.* Translated by Christian Preus. Saint Louis: Concordia, 2014.

Robinson, John. *The Pilgrim Spirit: Timeless Words of John Robinson.* Sundry Thoughts. December, 2019. newtestamentpattern.net

Rorty, Richard, ed. *The Linguistic Turn: Essays in Philosophical Method.* Chicago: University of Chicago Press, 1967.

Seddon, Fred. "Kant on Faith." *The Journal of Ayn Rand Studies.* 7, No. 1. University Park, Pa.: Penn State University, Press, 2005.

Sellers, R. V. *The Council of Chalcedon: A Historical and Doctrinal Survey.* London: SPCK, 1953.

1050 New Testament Commands. Christian Assemblies International: Coffs Harbour, NSW Australia, 2011. https://www.abc.net.au>reslib.

Bibliography

Vaughan, Thomas Ronald. *God and The Twelve Problems of Evil: Into Great Mystery.* Eugene, OR: Resource Publications, 2020.

———. *The Love of God and The Age to Come: No Eternal Hell.* Eugene OR: Wipf and Stock, 2019.

Ware, Kallistos. *The Orthodox Church.* London: Penguin, 1993.

Wittgenstein, Ludwig. *Philosophical Investigations.* Translated by G.E.M. Anscombe and Rush Rhees. New York: Macmillan, 1953.

———.*Tractatus Logico-Philosophicus.* Translated by Frank P. Ramsey and Charles Kay Ogden. Oxfordshire, UK: Kegan Paul, 1922.

Wrede, William. *The Messianic Secret.* Translated by Rev. James C. G. Greig. Cambridge: James Clark & Co., 1971.